The Hidden Faces of Courage

The Hidden Faces of Courage

Inspirational Stories About the Courage of Ordinary People

PETER C. WILCOX

RESOURCE *Publications* • Eugene, Oregon

THE HIDDEN FACES OF COURAGE
Inspirational Stories About the Courage of Ordinary People

Copyright © 2019 Peter C. Wilcox. All rights reserved. Except for brief quotations in critical publications or reviews, no part of this book may be reproduced in any manner without prior written permission from the publisher. Write: Permissions, Wipf and Stock Publishers, 199 W. 8th Ave., Suite 3, Eugene, OR 97401.

Resource Publications
An Imprint of Wipf and Stock Publishers
199 W. 8th Ave., Suite 3
Eugene, OR 97401

www.wipfandstock.com

PAPERBACK ISBN: 978-1-5326-7473-0
HARDCOVER ISBN: 978-1-5326-7474-7
EBOOK ISBN: 978-1-5326-7475-4

Manufactured in the U.S.A.   01/15/19

This book is dedicated to Mary, my mother, who died several years ago. Her quiet life of courage has allowed me to have a better understanding of this virtue and its importance in our lives. It is also dedicated to the many people I have worked with in my counseling career who have shown me the beauty and challenges of living a courageous life.

Contents

Introduction | ix

1. The Importance of Courage | 1

    A. Heroic Acts of Courage | 1

    B. The Quiet Life of Courage | 5

    C. Stories of Ordinary Courage | 7

2. Courage and our Personalities | 10

    A. The Courage to Live Authentically | 13

    B. The Courage to Accept and Love Ourselves | 20

    C. The Courage to Accept and Love People Who are Different from Us | 30

    D. The Courage to Face into Our Fears | 34

    E. The Courage to Face Our Limitations | 37

    F. The Courage To Forgive | 40

    G. The Courage To Grieve | 46

    H. The Courage to Become Angry | 51

    I. The Courage to Follow Our Dreams | 54

    J. The Courage to Live with Mystery | 57

    K. The Courage to Age Gracefully | 59

3. The Courage to "Let Go" | 66

    A. The Courage to Let Go of Our False Selves and Embrace Who We Are | 68

B. The Courage to Let Go of our Need for Approval | 73

  C. The Courage to Let Go of Comparison | 75

  D. The Courage to Let Go of Achievement as the Basis of our Self Worth | 80

  E. The Courage to Let Go of the "Lone Ranger Syndrome" | 83

  F. The Courage to Let Go of Our Need to be Right | 88

4. **Courage and the Challenges of Life** | 92

  A. The Courage to Live with Chronic Illness | 92

  B. The Courage of People Struggling with Mental Illness | 102

  C. The Courage of the Poor | 108

  D. The Courage to Live a Chaste Life | 113

  E. The Courage to Give "The More" | 116

Conclusion | 119

Bibliography | 121

Introduction

My mother died from Alzheimers disease several years ago. She was 92. As is often the case, it was a constant, insidious, slow moving disease, robbing her almost completely of her mental abilities at the end. For fifteen of the last seventeen years of her life, she lived with us. As her health and abilities slowly deteriorated over the years, we took care of her. I will always be eternally grateful to Margaret, my wife, for the love and care she gave to my mother. She took care of her like she was her own mother. Although she was still working full time, she always took care of my mother first. Bathing her, getting her dressed, feeding her, praying the rosary with her, were all part of the way she took care of her every day. For approximately the last two years, my mother's condition deteriorated to the point where she couldn't be left alone and needed twenty-four hour care. Although we tried to avoid this for as long as we could, my sister, brother and I finally decided she would receive the care she needed in a nursing home. Fortunately, we found one about four miles from our home, which allowed us to see her very often. Throughout these last two years, we always felt very blessed that my mother was somehow able to recognize us, probably up until the week before she died.

Reflecting back on these years, I have often wondered what my mother must have felt during these days. With the initial onset of this disease and during the earlier years when she could still talk, she would often say how difficult it was for her to cope. It was so frustrating for her to be losing her memory, to lose her ability to drive, to not remember people, and ultimately, to be unable to care for herself. As the disease progressed, she became more and more fearful and anxious.

However, during these years, I was also amazed at her strength and courage. The effort she put forth to remember things and do things for

Introduction

herself was nothing short of heroic. Her desire not to be a burden to us motivated her to try all the more.

There are so many people like my mother. They endure quietly, and with steadfast courage whatever comes their way in life. They are like the "anawim" in the Old Testament— the simple, good, kind people whom very few other people know about but who trust in the Lord. He is their strength. It is because of their faith in Him, that they live their lives with courage to face whatever comes their way. In over thirty-five years as a psychotherapist, I have often been amazed at the strength and courage of so many of my clients. Some have faced physical disabilities; others have struggled with mental, emotional, or psychological problems; still others with personal, family, or career issues. Some of their lives have been broken as they struggle each day with addiction issues. So often, their daily lives demand courage from them to face the reality of living each day.

These people are what I call "the hidden faces of courage." These are the courageous people I see every day. Often, not many people know of their struggles and courage. They certainly receive no notoriety or press. Yet they are always there, like my mother, doing the best they can each day, no matter what the challenge. It is for these people that I write these words. This book is dedicated to them. My hope is that they will know that their strength and courage are seen and appreciated, and that they will know that their daily struggles are meaningful and life-giving. And, if more of us could understand the courage of others, if we could simply "walk in their shoes," the more we could, hopefully, appreciate the people around us who might struggle with issues that we might not ever know about.

1

The Importance of Courage

"Courage doesn't always roar. Sometimes, courage is the little voice at the end of the day that says I'll try again tomorrow." Mary Ann Radmacher

"WE BECOME BRAVE BY doing brave acts," observed Aristotle in his *Nicomachean Ethics*. "Dispositions of character, virtues and vices, are progressively fixed in us through practice. Thus, by being habituated to despise things that are terrible and to stand our ground against them we become brave, and it is when we have become so that we shall be most able to stand our ground against them."[1]

A. Heroic Acts of Courage

The brave person is not one who is never afraid. Being afraid is a perfectly appropriate emotion when confronted with fearful things. The great American novelist Herman Melville makes the Aristotelian point beautifully in a telling passage in *Moby Dick*, when Starbuck, the chief mate of the Pequod, first addresses the crew. "I will have no man in my boat," said Starbuck, "who is not afraid of a whale."[2]

For most people, it is relatively easy to recognize heroic acts of courage which continue to inspire us. Take for example, Rosa Parks, refusing to give

---

1. Aristotle, *Nicomachean Ethics,* Book II, ch. 1.
2. Melville, *Moby Dick,* 112.

up her seat on the bus; Harriett Tubman, leading slaves to freedom on the underground railroad; Martin Luther King Jr., standing up for civil rights; the police, firefighters, and citizens who rushed into buildings to save lives on September 11, 2001; those on flight 93, who stormed the cockpit of the airplane on that same day and sent it crashing in a field in PA, rather than allow it to head back to Washington, D.C. These acts, and so many similar ones, demand a tremendous amount of courage to stand up for a moral principle.

The late John McCain, in his book *Why Courage Matters*, tells the story of special forces master sergeant Roy Benavidez, whose bravery is almost too difficult to comprehend. Roy was the son of a Texas sharecropper and orphaned at a young age. He was a quiet boy who was mistaken as slow, and teased as a dumb Mexican by his classmates. He left school in the eighth grade to work in the cotton fields. At nineteen, he joined the army. On his first tour in Vietnam, in 1964, he stepped on a land mine. Army doctors thought the wound would be permanently crippling. It wasn't. He recovered and became a Green Beret.

During his second combat tour, in the early morning of May 2, 1968, in Loc Ninh, Vietnam, sergeant Benavidez monitored by radio a twelve man reconnaissance patrol. Three Green Berets, friends of his, and nine Montagnard tribesmen had been dropped in the dense jungle west of Loc Ninh, just inside Cambodia. No man aboard the low-flying helicopters beating noisily toward the landing zone that morning could have been aware of how dangerous the assignment was. Considered an enemy sanctuary, the area was known to be vigilantly patrolled by a sizable force of the North Vietnamese army. Once on the ground, the twelve men were almost immediately engaged by the enemy and soon surrounded by a large force that grew to a battalion.

The mission had been a mistake, and three helicopters were ordered to evacuate the besieged patrol. Fierce small arms and antiaircraft fire, wounding several crew members, forced the helicopters to return to their base. Listening on the radio, Benavidez heard one of his friends scream, "get us out of here." He jumped into one of the returning helicopters, volunteering for a second evacuation attempt. When he arrived at the scene, he found that none of the patrol had made it to the landing zone. Four were already dead, including the team leader, and the other eight were wounded and unable to move. Carrying a knife and a medic bag, Benavidez made the sign of the cross, leapt from the helicopter hovering ten feet off the ground,

The Importance of Courage

and ran seventy yards to his injured comrades. Before he reached them, he was shot in the leg, face, and head. He got up and kept moving.

When he reached their position, he armed himself with an enemy rifle, began to treat the wounded, reposition them, distribute ammunition, and call in air strikes. He threw smoke grenades to indicate their location and ordered the helicopter pilot to come in close to pick up the wounded. He dragged four of the wounded aboard, and then, while under intense fire and returning fire with his captured weapon, he ran alongside the helicopter as it flew just a few feet off the ground toward the others. He got the rest of the wounded aboard, as well as the dead, except for the fallen team leader. As he raced to retrieve his body, and the classified documents the dead soldier had carried, he was shot in the stomach and grenade fragments cut into his back.

Before he could make his way back toward the helicopter, the pilot was fatally wounded and the aircraft crashed upside down. He helped the wounded escape the burning wreckage and organized them in a defensive perimeter. He called for air strikes and fire from circling gunships to suppress the ever increasing enemy fire enough to allow another evacuation attempt. Critically wounded, Benavidez moved constantly along the perimeter, bringing water and ammunition to the defenders, treating their wounds, encouraging them to hold on. He sustained several more gunshot wounds, but he continued to fight. For six hours.

When another helicopter landed, he helped the wounded toward it, one and two at a time. On his second trip, an enemy soldier ran up behind him and struck him with his rifle butt. Sergeant Benavidez turned and fought the man with his bayonet, hand to hand, to the death. Wounded again, he then made his way back to collect the classified documents before at last climbing aboard and collapsing, apparently dead.

The army doctor back at the base thought he was dead anyway. Bleeding profusely, his intestines spilling from his stomach wounds, completely immobile, and unable to speak, they flew him back to Saigon for surgery, where he began a year in hospitals recovering from seven serious gunshot wounds, twenty-eight shrapnel wounds, and bayonet wounds in both arms.[3]

Hard to believe, isn't it, what this one man did? What kind of training prepares you to do that? What kind of unit solidarity, how great the love and trust for the man to your right and your left, inspires you to the

---

3. McCain, *Why Courage Matters*, 4–8.

superhuman heroics of Roy Benavidez? How does one ever acquire this kind of courage?

The great English statesman, Winston Churchill, said that courage is the first of human qualities because it guarantees all the others.[4] Existentialist philosopher Soren Kierkegaard pointed out that courage isn't the absence of despair and fear but the capacity to move ahead in spite of them.[5]

Sometimes courage involves standing up for your beliefs and convictions. This is the way it was for Sir Thomas More. It was July 6, 1535. He had been a prisoner in the tower of London for over a year. It was now time for his execution. When he came out to mount the steps to the scaffold, he said to the officials, in a rather humorous way, "I pray you, Mr. Lieutenant, see me safe up and for my coming down, I can shift for myself." While he was on the scaffold, More said that he died, "the king's good servant, but God's first."[6]

Sir Thomas More (1478–1535), was an English lawyer, author, statesman, and councillor to Henry VIII. More opposed the king's separation from the Catholic Church and refused to acknowledge him as supreme head of the Church of England. He also refused to acknowledge Henry's marriage annulment from Catherine of Aragon and his subsequent marriage to Anne Boleyn. Tried for treason for refusing to take the Oath of Supremacy which would have made the king the supreme head of the English Church, he was convicted and beheaded. Sir Thomas More was canonized by the Catholic Church in 1933 and today is the patron saint of lawyers.

Mother Teresa said, "to have courage for whatever comes in life—everything lies in that."[7] Fortunately, most of us don't have to face the reality of risking our lives like Sergeant Roy Benavidez or have the kind of courage that enabled Sir Thomas More to give his life for a moral principle. We might not even have the kind of courage that is needed that will have a huge impact on the lives of others. But if what Mother Teresa said is true, and I think that it is, then each of us will have many opportunities to be courageous our own ways. These people and their heroic acts of courage can inspire us to be courageous when our opportunities arise.

---

4. https://www.brainyquote.com/author/winston_churchill.
5. https://www.azquotes.com/author/8000-soren_kierkegaard.
6. Quoted from brainyquote.com/thomasmore.html.
7. Quoted from http.//statusmind.com/life-quotes.html.

B. The Quiet Life of Courage

When I was a young boy, I remember being scared at times because in the bedroom I shared with my brother, there was a closet. Sometimes, the closet door would be left open at night and our clothes hanging up on a hook. For some reason, our clothes at times would be shaped in such a way that they looked like very scary monsters to me. I can remember crying and calling out for my mother. She would come to me, comfort me and show me there were no monsters. There was no need to be afraid.

Each of us can be afraid of things in life in our own way. For some, it can be clothes looking like monsters in a closet. Or, the fear of failure or standing up for our convictions. For others, it might be the fear of illness or dying. For still others, it might be our fear of speaking up to our friends if we were worried about some detrimental or dangerous behaviors they were engaged in. Each of us can be afraid in our own way. Fear comes in many colors.

That is why the virtue of courage is so important. It touches on so many dimensions of life. Courage comes from the Latin word "cor," which means heart. Some people believe that courage is the ability to do something that you know is difficult or dangerous. Others define courage as the ability to do what a person believes is right, like standing up for your convictions, especially in the face of criticism. However, no matter how we might define courage, it is important to remember that there are no small acts of courage. You can't compare the courage it takes to battle cancer with the courage it takes to become a doctor. Both are very brave acts. You can't compare the courage it takes to become an Olympian with the courage it takes to raise a physically or mentally challenged child. Both acts are heroic. Courage comes in many sizes and shapes.

As I wrote in the previous chapter, we can think of courage in a big way—like someone risking their life to save another person or perhaps first responders who are always there risking their lives to protect us. But courage is a much richer idea than this. Over the years, in my counseling practice, I have come to understand that many people are extremely courageous in a quiet, unassuming way. However, they get no press, no notoriety. No one ever writes about them. But, if Mother Teresa is correct in saying that having courage is important to each of us for whatever we have to face in life, then we can begin to capture the importance of this virtue.

Consider, for a moment, the courage it requires on a daily basis to face an illness or addiction. Or, the courage it takes "to speak the truth in love," as St. Paul said, to someone about an issue or behavior that is wrong or unhealthy when doing this might jeopardize a long time friendship. Or, in the business world, what about the courage it takes to refuse to participate in an unethical practice when it might cost a person their job. There is even a great deal of courage involved in our willingness to work on ourselves—to rid ourselves of our masks, our false selves, as the spiritual writer Thomas Merton says. This kind of willingness to die to ourselves and our selfishness often requires a healthy dose of courage. Spiritual writer and psychologist Rollo May wrote, "in human beings courage is necessary to make being and becoming possible."[8] It takes courage and a lot of hard work to become who you are meant to be. Thomas Keating, a Trappist monk and spiritual writer, expresses our calling: "the greatest accomplishment in life is to be what we are, which is God's idea of what He wanted us to be when He brought us into being. . . . Accepting that gift is accepting God's will for us, and in its acceptance is found the path to growth and ultimate fulfillment."[9] Courage can become a quiet part of our lives in so many ways.

Perhaps one of the most courageous groups of people that many of us know about but often do not connect with courage are the people who take care of others—caretakers. There are so many hidden faces of courage among these groups of people who quietly go about their work of taking care of others each day with love and devotion. Paul and Mary are two of these courageous people who have cared for both of their daughters for over thirty years. Both girls were born with Spina Bifida, a devastating illness that happens when a baby is in the womb and the spinal column does not completely close. As is often the case, both daughters faced many disabilities and needed twenty-four hour care. After much reflection and prayer, Paul and Mary decided they would take care of their daughters at home. They did this for over thirty years. Can we ever begin to imagine the love and devotion of these two parents? Can we ever grasp the strength and courage required of them to care for both daughters each and every day? This is just one example of caretakers who live a quiet life of courage. And maybe we can learn from Paul and Mary about what it means to live a quiet life of courage as the opportunities arise for us.

---

8. May, *The Courage to Create*, 4.
9. Keating, *The Heart of the World*, 69.

THE IMPORTANCE OF COURAGE

C. Stories of Ordinary Courage

Everyone wants to be brave. In one of its earliest forms, the word *courage* had a very different definition than it does today. Courage originally meant "to speak one's mind by telling all one's heart." Over time, this definition has changed and today courage is more synonymous with being heroic. Heroics are important and we certainly need heroes, but I think we've lost touch with the idea that speaking honestly and openly about who we are, about what we're feeling, and about our experiences, both good and bad, is also included in the definition of courage. Heroics is often about putting our life on the line. Ordinary courage is about putting our vulnerability on the line. In today's world that's pretty extraordinary.

When we pay attention, we can see courage every day. We see it when people reach out for help. For a number of years, I was fortunate enough to teach at several universities in the graduate school programs of theology and pastoral counseling. I have seen ordinary courage in my classroom when a student raises her/his hand and says, "I'm completely lost. I have no idea what you're talking about." Do you know how incredibly brave it is to say "I don't know" especially in graduate school when you're pretty sure everyone around you gets it? Of course, in my years of teaching, I know that if one person can find the courage to say, "you've lost me," there are probably at least ten more students who feel exactly the same way. They may not take the risk, but they certainly benefit from that one person's courage.

One of my clients told me about a courageous thing her youngest daughter did. Her daughter, Jenny, who was eight, had gone to a slumber party. About 10:30 p m , my client received a phone call that said, "Mom, can you come get me?" When Jenny's mother went to pick her up, Jenny got in the car and said, "I'm sorry. I just wasn't brave enough. I got homesick. It was so hard. Everyone was asleep, and I had to walk to Mary's mom's bedroom and wake her up."

As they pulled into their driveway, the mom got out of the car and walked around to the back seat where Jenny was sitting. She got in the car, sat next to her and said, "Jenny I think asking for what you need is one of the bravest things you will ever do. I suffered through a couple of really miserable sleepovers and slumber parties because I was too afraid to ask to go home. I'm very proud of you."

The next morning during breakfast, Jenny said, "I thought about what you said last night. Can I be brave again and ask for something else?" Her mother smiled. "I have another slumber party next weekend. Would you be willing to pick me up at bedtime? I'm just not ready." That's courage. The kind we could all use more of.

I also see courage in myself when I am willing to risk being vulnerable and disappointed. Since my retirement several years ago, I have been writing books and articles. Fortunately, I have been able to get many of the things I have written, published. But over the years, I have noticed that if I really wanted something to happen—like a book manuscript I sent to a publishing company, to be accepted—I would pretend that it didn't matter that much. If a friend or colleague would ask, "are you excited about getting your book published?" I would shrug it off and say, "Oh, it's not that big of a deal." Of course, in reality, I was clearly hoping and praying that it would happen.

It's only been in the last few years as I have delved more deeply into this idea of courage, that I have learned that playing down the exciting stuff doesn't take the pain away if my manuscript would be rejected. It does, however, minimize the joy when it does happen. It also creates a lot of isolation. Once you have diminished the importance of something, your friends are not likely to call and say "I'm sorry that didn't work out. I know you were excited about it."

Now, when someone asks me about getting a manuscript published, I try to pay attention to how I am actually feeling and practice courage and say, "I'm very excited about the possibility of having my manuscript accepted. I'm trying to stay realistic, but I really hope it happens." When things haven't panned out, it's been comforting to be able to say to my wife or a friend, "remember that manuscript I told you about? It was turned down and I feel so disappointed."

Recently, I also read about another story of ordinary courage at a preschool where Linda's son was a student. Parents were invited to attend a holiday music presentation put on by the kids. You know the scene— twenty-five children singing with fifty-plus parents, grandparents, and siblings in the audience holding forty-one cell phones and video cameras. The parents were holding up their cameras in the air and randomly snapping pictures while they scrambled to make sure that their kids knew they were there and on time.

In addition to all the commotion in the audience, one three year old girl, who was new to the class, cried her way through the entire performance because she couldn't see her mom from the makeshift stage. As it turns out, her mother got stuck in traffic and missed the entire performance. By the time her mother arrived, Linda was kneeling by the classroom door telling her son good-bye. From her low vantage point, Linda watched the little girl's mother burst through the door and immediately start scanning the room to find her daughter. Just as Linda was getting ready to stand up and point her toward the back of the classroom where a teacher was holding her daughter, another mother walked by us, looked straight at the stressed mom, shook her head, and rolled her eyes.

Linda stood up, took a deep breath, and tried to reason with the part of her that wanted to chase after the better-than-you, self-righteous, eye-rolling mom and give her a piece of her mind. Just then, two more moms walked up to this now tearful mother and smiled. One of the mother's put her hand on top of the woman's shoulder and said, "we've all been there. I missed the last one. I wasn't just late. I completely forgot. I missed the whole thing." Linda watched as the woman's face softened and she wiped away a tear. The second woman looked at her and said, "my son was the only one who wasn't wearing pajamas on PJ day—he still tells me that it was the most rotten day ever. It will be okay. We're all in the same boat."

By the time this mother made it to the back of the room where the teacher was still comforting her daughter, she looked calm. Something that I'm sure came in handy when her daughter ran toward her and jumped in her arms.. The moms who stopped and shared their stories of imperfection and vulnerability were practicing courage. They took the time to stop and say, "Here's my story. You're not alone." They didn't have to stop and share. They could have easily joined the perfect parent parade and marched right by her.

As these stories illustrate, ordinary courage has a ripple effect. Every time we choose courage, we make everyone around us a little better and the world a little braver. And our world could stand to be a little kinder and braver.

2

Courage and our Personalities

"The Longest Journey is the Journey Inward" Dag Hammarskjold

WE MAY NOT MAKE the connection between courage and our personalities, but in some interesting ways, I have often seen how these two dimensions of our lives are intimately connected. What might be an easy thing to do for some people, might require a great deal of courage from someone else. For example, an extrovert might find it very easy and actually be energized by going into a room full of people they don't know, introduce themselves and carry on a conversation and truly enjoy it. On the other hand, an introvert might be able to do this, but won't particularly enjoy it or be energized by it. It can take courage for this person to make themselves walk into this type of situation.

Some years ago, one of my clients was a young business man who had recently been diagnosed with cancer. He came to see me because he was mostly concerned with how his wife would be able to manage both his illness and the possibility of his death. He described her as painfully shy and retiring, almost fragile. They had even eloped because she could not face having a public ceremony. He could not imagine how she would be able to deal with their children and with his very successful business by herself.

When I first met her, she was very much as he said. Yet as he struggled with his cancer treatments and eventually died prematurely, she underwent a remarkable change. It was she who supported him in taking risks,

Courage and our Personalities

even calling doctors and other experts all over the country. It was she who took over more and more of his business, learning as she went along. Most importantly, it was she who supported and comforted their children. Her courage, in both her personal and her business life, was as awesome as it was unexpected. By the time he died, she was running the business and afterwards continued to make a success of it alone.

A few years after her husband died, she called me for an appointment. She wanted to discuss some decisions about her children's education and ask me if her husband had indicated any opinions that might serve as guidance for her now. The person who came to visit me was not the woman I had met only three years before. I commented on the changes and on the remarkable strength and courage she had shown in dealing with her husband's illness and death and in making her own life. I asked her if she had known that she would be able to do the things she had done in the past few years.

"Well, no," she said. She went on to say that she had always been shy, and been labeled by others as shy from the time she was a small girl. So, no one had ever challenged her and she had never challenged herself. Yet her courage and her ability to take risks had come very naturally to her. She had been surprised at first, but then she had decided that her courage was because of her shyness. She smiled and went on to say, "I was so shy that it took courage for me to say hello to someone, it took courage to go to the grocery store and to the cleaners, it felt like a risk every time I answered the telephone. It took a lot of courage just to live, to do the things that other people do without thinking every day. I guess over the years my courage just grew from being used all the time like that. And when the time came that Joe needed me so badly, when I could no longer help him and be shy, why, I guess I was ready."

In a sense, we are all more than we know. Wholeness is never lost, it is only forgotten. Integrity rarely means that we need to add something to ourselves. Often, it is more an undoing than a doing, a freeing ourselves from beliefs we have about who we are and ways we have been persuaded to "fix" ourselves to know who we genuinely are. Like my client, even after many years of seeing, thinking, and living one way, we are able to reach past all that to claim our integrity and live in a way we may never have expected to live.

Integrity is the only path in life upon which you will never get lost. Placing integrity at the cornerstone of every decision you make requires a willingness to do what is right above what is convenient. And this takes courage. At times, this means veering off the safe and comfortable path onto a less traveled one where the risk of failure or disapproval may run high. At other times, it calls you to forge your own path.

Robert Frost expresses the challenge and importance of choosing this less traveled path so well in his poem *The Road Not Taken*.

> Two roads diverged in a yellow wood,
> And sorry I could not travel both
> And be one traveler, long I stood
> And Looked down one as far as I could
> To where it bent in the undergrowth;
> Then took the other, as just as fair,
> And having perhaps the better claim,
> Because it was grassy and wanted wear;
> Though as for that the passing there
> Had worn them really about the same.
>
> And both that morning equally lay
> In leaves no step had trodden black.
> Oh, I kept the first for another day!
> Yet knowing how way leads on to way,
> I doubted if I should ever come back.
>
> I shall be telling this with a sigh
> Somewhere ages and ages hence:
> Two roads diverged in a wood, and I—
> I took the one less traveled by,
> And that has made all the difference.[1]

At its core, integrity is about wholeness and alignment between your deepest values, what you are doing and who you are being in the world. Integrity calls forth living with courage. It calls forth greatness.

Sometimes, our personalities as well as our experiences, can also make us feel that we are very unimportant in life and believe that what we do with our lives is not very meaningful. But this is simply not the case. Some years ago, another one of my clients shared an early personality struggle with me.

---

1. https://www.poets.org/poem/road-not-taken.

When she was younger, she said that it had taken her a long time to realize that she had an impact on the people around her. For years, she too suffered from shyness and a lack of self-esteem. She felt as though she was invisible to others and that her presence or absence had little or no positive influence on anyone. As a young adult, she would often not respond to a written invitation or return a phone message. Sometimes, she would leave a party without a word to anyone, including the host or hostess. It simply never occurred to her that anyone might notice that she had not responded or that she was no longer there. Years later, she was stunned to discover that all those years she had been seen as aloof and rude and that her behavior often hurt people. She certainly had never meant to do that. However, she felt so badly about herself, she truly believed that her presence didn't matter.

Many people are like this client of mine. Because of their personalities, they don't believe that they make a difference in life. But it is so important to believe in ourselves and to know that our presence always makes a difference. Sir Thomas Browne wrote: "we carry within us the wonders we seek without us."[2] We all have the power to affect others, probably more than we realize. Having the courage to believe in ourselves allows us to live each day believing that we can always make a difference.

Most of us tend to look outside of ourselves for heroes and teachers. It has not occurred to many people that they may already be the role model they seek. The courage and wholeness they are looking for may be trapped within their personalities by beliefs, attitudes, and self-doubt. But our wholeness exists in us now. Trapped though it may be, it can be called upon for guidance, direction, and most fundamentally, comfort. It can be remembered. Eventually, we may come to live by it.

A. The Courage to Live Authentically

In Margery William's little book, entitled *The Velveteen Rabbit,* there is a lovely dialogue between the Skin Horse and the Rabbit. The wise character in the story is the Skin Horse who is trying to help the Rabbit learn how to become real.

> What is Real? asked the Rabbit one day. Does it mean having things that buzz inside you and a stick-out handle?

---

2. Quoted from brainyquote.com/sirthomasbrowne.html.

Real isn't how you are made, said the Skin Horse. It's a thing that happens to you. When a child loves you for a long, long time, not just to play with, but REALLY loves you, then you become Real.

Does it hurt? asked the Rabbit.

Sometimes, said the Skin Horse, for he was always truthful. When you are Real you don't mind being hurt.

Does it happen all at once, like being wound up, he asked, or bit by bit?

It doesn't happen all at once, said the Skin Horse. You become. It takes a long time. That's why it doesn't often happen to people who break easily, or have sharp edges, or who have to be carefully kept. Generally, by the time you are Real, most of your hair has been loved off, and your eyes drop out and you get loose in the joints and very shabby. But these things don't matter at all, because once you are Real you can't be ugly, except to people who don't understand.[3]

Maybe one of the most challenging things for all of us is to become Real—to become our own person that God created us to be with all our own uniqueness, beauty, and individual qualities. It's something that we work on every day of our lives in one way or another. Using our gifts and talents, making choices each day are all part of this process, to become our own person and live authentically. Soren Kierkegaard reminds us how important this is when he writes, "the most common form of despair is not being who you are."[4]

When I was younger, I used to think that people were either authentic or inauthentic. Authenticity was simply a quality that you had or that you were lacking. I think that is probably the way most of us use the term: "she's a very authentic person." But over the years, my clients have taught me that, like many desirable ways of being, authenticity is not something we have or don't have. It's a practice—a conscious choice of how we want to live. Often, people attempt to live their lives backwards: they try to have more things, or more money, in order to do more of what they want so that they will be happier. But, in my experience, the way it actually works is the reverse. You must first be who you really are, then do what you really need to do, in order to have what you want.

3. Williams, *The Velveteen Rabbit*, 5.
4. https://www.azquotes.com/author/8000-soren_kierkegaard.

Courage and our Personalities

Authenticity is really the daily practice of letting go of who we think we're supposed to be and embracing who we are. It's really a collection of choices that we have to make every day. It's about the choice to show up and be real. The choice to be honest. The choice to let our true selves be seen. The choice to cultivate the courage to be imperfect and to allow ourselves to be vulnerable.

There are people who consciously practice being authentic, there are people who don't, and there are the rest of us who are authentic on some days and not so authentic on other days.

The idea that we can choose authenticity makes most of us feel both hopeful and exhausted. We feel hopeful because being real is something we value. Most of us are drawn to warm, down-to-earth, honest people, and we want to be like that in our own lives. But we can also feel exhausted because most of us know that choosing authenticity in a culture that dictates everything from how much we are supposed to weigh to what our homes are supposed to look like is a huge undertaking.

Choosing authenticity is not an easy choice and it requires courage. E.E. Cummings said, "to be nobody-but-yourself in a world which is doing its best, night and day, to make you everybody but yourself—means to fight the hardest battle which any human being can fight—and never stop fighting."[5] "Staying real" is one of the most courageous battles that we will ever fight.

Some years ago, I was leading a retreat and in one of our sessions I asked the participants to take a sheet of paper and make two lists of twenty-one values that were important to them. On the first list, they were to rank these values according to what was most important to them in their work, and then on the second list to rank them according to what was most important to them personally. The list included values such as admiration, control, wisdom, competence, compassion, happiness, fame, success, power, love, and kindness.

It was interesting to discover that none of those who participated in this exercise made two identical lists, and often the two lists were strikingly different. Kindness, for example, might be number two on someone's list of personal values and number fifteen on their list of desirable work values. Competence might be someone's number one professional value and come in dead last on their personal list. Many people were puzzled and dismayed to discover that they lived their personal lives in one way

---

5. E.E.Cummings Quotes,goodreads.com/author/quotes/10547.

and their professional lives in quite another. This exercise had made them consciously aware of this difference for the first time. As we discussed these results, a surprising number of people said that they did not think that it was possible to both live and work by the values that were personally important to them. As one man put it, "life diminishes you." But, as another person said, "only with your permission."

What was true for these retreatants is probably true for all of us. The experience of sacrificing authenticity and integrity is one that many people struggle with on a daily basis. Over the years, numerous people have told me in a variety of ways that they felt they could not be authentic out of fear of rejection or some other form of loss or because they find themselves living and working with people who see things very differently than they do. They have become invisible in order to survive or maintain the status quo. This is why courage is required to go "against the grain," so to speak. Nevertheless, when we don't live authentically with ourselves, something begins to erode inside of us. We may survive, but we will never be whole or fully alive.

Many people these days talk about the high level of stress that they experience. But perhaps losing integrity with yourself is the greatest stress of all, far more hurtful to us than competition, time pressures, or lack of respect. Our vitality is rooted in our integrity. Becoming separated from our authentic values weakens us. This may be why, when people's lives are challenged by a serious illness and they instinctively begin to gather their strength, their values are often among the first things that change.

It is difficult to live authentically, to be a person of integrity. And it takes courage. Most of us wear masks. We may have worn them for so long that we have forgotten that we have put them on. Sometimes, our culture may even try to demand that we wear them. Many of us have learned to cover over what is most authentic in ourselves in order to protect ourselves or gain the approval of others. We may have lived this way for so long that we have lost our authentic self. It is important in life to understand what masks we wear that cover over who we truly are and to let go of the life long roles and self expectations that we have assumed. These are ways of living that are not genuinely our own.

When I first met Kathy, her psychology practice was barely surviving. She shared offices with a group of physicians, and desperate to be accepted and work under what she perceived as the umbrella of their credibility, she took whatever crumbs fell from their professional table. Hers was the

Courage and our Personalities

smallest office in the building and hers was the only name not listed on the office door. It was obvious to me from the beginning how dedicated and gifted a therapist she was. However, this compromising attitude troubled me, although I didn't say anything about it at the time. But Kathy felt validated by the association and she was convinced that she needed referrals from the doctors in order to have clients.

Kathy was a shy person, a little apologetic and sometimes hesitant in trying to find the right words in a conversation. She was also just the slightest bit clumsy. However, all this actually made her very endearing. You somehow felt at home with her and safe. Her clients loved her.

One day she told me she was moving from her present office. Although I was pleased, I asked her why she had decided to leave. "They don't have wheelchair access," she said. I guess I looked surprised so she went on to say that she had not told me everything about herself. She continued to tell her story and said that years ago when she was young, she had a very serious stroke and was not expected to recover. "I was astonished," I said. "I had no idea." She replied, "nobody does." I went on to ask her why she had kept this part of her life a secret. Almost in tears, she said that for years she had felt damaged and ashamed. "I wanted to put it behind me," she said. "I thought if I could be seen as normal I would be more than I was." And so she guarded her secret closely. Neither her colleagues nor her clients knew. She had felt certain that others would not refer to her or want to come to her for help if they knew. However, she was no longer sure this was true.

"So what do you plan to do now?" I asked her. She looked down at her hands in her lap. "I think I will just be myself," she told me. "I will see people like myself. People who are not like others. People who have had strokes and other brain injuries. People who can never be normal again. I think I can help them be whole." Over the past eight years, Kathy has become widely known for her work. She has been honored by several community groups and interviewed in newspapers. She often speaks on these kinds of topics and consults for businesses and hospitals. The many people she has helped refer others to her. Her practice is thriving. Her own name is now on the door. All Kathy needed in order to be authentic was the courage to truly be herself.

In the New Testament, the apostle Andrew has always been a wonderful example of an authentic person for me. There are three glimpses of Andrew that we are given in John's Gospel. The first time that Andrew appears is when he brings his brother Simon Peter to Jesus. Having discovered the Messiah for himself, through John the Baptist, Andrew wastes no time in informing his brother about Jesus and arranging an interview. Andrew's transparency is reflected in the simplicity of the language used to describe the incident. "[Andrew] first found his brother Simon and told him, 'we have found the Messiah.' Then he brought him to Jesus" (John 1: 41–42).

The second time Andrew appears is in John 6: 8. On this occasion, Andrew presents a little boy with five barley loaves to the Lord. The situation is a large, hungry crowd and no apparent means of feeding them. Andrew seems to agonize over the problem: "there is a boy here who has five barley loaves and two fish; but what good are these for so many?" What does Andrew do? He acts. He leads the child with the loaves forward and leaves the rest to Christ. Again, it was Andrew who brought the little boy to Jesus. He trusted that the Lord would take care of the situation.

The last occasion is in John 12: 20–23, just before Christ's Passion. Some Greeks arrive in Jerusalem anxious to see Jesus. They run into Philip who takes them straight to Andrew. Evidently, by this time, Andrew had a reputation of knowing what to do when others came seeking. Certainly, Philip had learned to trust Andrew from the previous incident.

Together, they take the Greeks to Jesus. Their arrival is not unexpected. Recognizing here the Gentiles who will form his church, Jesus proclaims, "the hour has come." This is the hour of the cross. This is the hour of the world's redemption.

Andrew is never mentioned again in John's Gospel. With his objective of bringing others to the Lord accomplished, he is content to remain in the shadows. Andrew is clearly a biblical person who, by his life, gives us a deeper understanding of what authenticity is all about. On every occasion that he appears in John's Gospel, Andrew is shown bringing someone to Jesus and then quietly retiring to let the Lord complete his work in that person.

Andrew never draws attention to himself, but to Jesus. He is a reminder to us that an authentic person ought to be transparent because we are to serve the Lord and not ourselves. It is interesting to see that we lose sight altogether of Andrew since he gives way so perfectly to Christ and the other person every time. What is admirable about Andrew for me is that he truly knew himself and realized that his role was to lead others to the Lord. Similarly, we grow in authenticity when we truly know ourselves and are comfortable with ourselves—when we become transparent. Otherwise, we will get in the way of bringing others to Jesus.

Courage and our Personalities

There is something very appealing about a truly authentic person. Maybe this is because we don't meet this type of person very often. Andrew was truly free to be himself. He didn't have to play a role, wear a mask or pretend he was someone else. He was simply himself and was comfortable with that. Moreover, authenticity is often manifested through the kind of transparency that Andrew possessed.

In his personal diary, which he entitled *Markings*, Dag Hammarskjold, Secretary-General of the United Nations in the 1950's, reflected on this idea of authenticity and transparency in his own life and ministry. He wrote about how he never wanted to get in the way of bringing others to Jesus. Using the images of a *mirror* and a *doorway*, he prayed for the grace of never becoming a mirror in which he reflected his own image back to other people, but rather a doorway through which people could walk in order to catch a better glimpse of Jesus. He once prayed, "who will give me the power to transform the mirror into a doorway?"[6]

Becoming more authentic and transparent in our own lives—like Andrew and Hammarskjold—allows us to become more of a doorway through which the people we minister to and come in contact with each day can catch a clearer image of Jesus. And, like Andrew and Hammarskjold, an authentic person is not selfish, not focused on oneself, and doesn't want to make ourselves the center of attention. It doesn't desire that we become better known. In fact, it doesn't even need to be successful in the eyes of the world. Rather, an authentic person invites us to become a doorway and wants people to look through them in order to point the way to Jesus.

Andrew is a mature adult, secure in himself, comfortable in his own skin, and clear about his mission. He does not allow jealously, ambition or pettiness to obstruct the gift of grace that flows between Jesus and the person. Once the connection has been made, he steps aside. He can do this because he has no illusions about himself. He is not the Messiah—Jesus is.

It is also interesting to see that later, when Peter is entrusted with the keys of the kingdom and made chief shepherd of the flock, Andrew makes no complaint that he has been passed over. There is no whining, no resentment, no anger, no bitter claim that he met Jesus first. Andrew understands his role. He is content to have created that space for Christ and for others in which his brother can reach the Lord and grow in his call to holiness.

Authenticity places service above self-interest. It requires that we struggle with the illusions that we have about ourselves or that can come

---

6. Hammarskjold, *Markings*, 83.

to us from other people. Often these illusions can be very enticing and can actually keep us from bringing others to the Lord as Andrew did. Authenticity is the antidote to pride and to every urge to dominate or possess or manipulate just to maintain one's image or protect one's status in the community. Feeling secure in themselves, they allow and encourage others to be who they truly are.

Authenticity is an ongoing process, a dynamic happening over time that requires our ongoing attention. Often, it requires courage. There is probably no better way to spend our time.

B. The Courage to Accept and Love Ourselves

It requires a lot of courage to let go of who we think we are supposed to be and embrace who we truly are—warts and all. We all struggle with shame and guilt and the fear of "not being good enough." Many of us are afraid to let our true selves be seen and known.

Susan was plagued with self-doubt. But it made no sense. She was a straight A student through college and the seminary. She was a beloved associate pastor at a thriving congregation. Her parishioners found her bright and articulate, personal and caring. And yet, a basic fear all but paralyzed her when she was asked to preach, facilitate a meeting or teach an adult education course. An inner voice of self-doubt eroded her ability to speak in front of people. This critical inner voice constantly said to her "who do you think you are? You've got nothing worth saying to these people. You're a fraud. And surely this time, they will see it."

Like Susan, many of us struggle to accept and love ourselves. We can be callous to our own suffering. So often, we scrutinize and pick at our faults and imperfections. We often seem to have a negative tape playing constantly in our head saying things like: "what a disgrace you are. What you said was awful. How could you possibly think such horrible things? You don't have what it takes. That's not nearly good enough. What is wrong with you? When are you going to get it together?" And on and on. Most of us would never attack another person with these kinds of words that we use on ourselves.

After working with Susan for several months, I asked her one day, "where did you learn this way of talking to yourself?" And then she remembered. When she was thirteen years old, she took first place in a school speech contest. She rushed home, eager to share her triumph with her father. Her dad, however, was in one of his moods. As she bounced into the den waving her trophy, her dad just scowled and said, "who do you think you are? Don't be throwing that trophy in my face. You got nothing to say. Never did. Nobody wants to listen to you." Susan was cut to the bone. She fled to her bedroom. Then she threw the trophy in the trash.

Susan's father had shamed her into believing that she was a bad person who couldn't do anything right. And this kind of shame is one of the major barriers to accepting and loving ourselves. In Jungian circles, shame is often referred to as the "swampland of the soul." When we feel ashamed, we struggle to believe in our own goodness. Sometimes, we can even have what I call "shame tapes" rummaging around in our heads. These are the messages that make us feel like we are "never good enough." When these tapes start playing, they often say things like,

"What will people think?"

"You can't *really* love yourself yet. You're not pretty enough, skinny enough, or talented enough."

"I'm going to pretend that everything is ok."

"No one can find out about this part of my life."

"I'll change to fit in if I have to."

"Who do you think you are to put your thoughts, ideas, beliefs, writing out in the world?"

Shame is that warm feeling that washes over us, making us feel small, flawed, and never good enough. It is basically the fear of being unlovable—the total opposite of accepting and loving ourselves. One definition I like says that "shame is the intensely painful feeling or experience of believing that we are flawed and therefore unworthy of love and belonging."[7] Shame keeps loving ourselves at a distance by convincing us that owning our own story of who we are will lead to people thinking less of us. Shame is all about fear. We're afraid that people won't like us if they know the truth about who we are, where we come from, what we believe or how much we're struggling.

Sometimes, people want to believe that shame is reserved for the folks who have survived terrible traumas. While this is often true, shame is also something we all experience. To feel shame is to be human. When we have worked hard to make sure everything looks "just right" on the outside, the stakes are high when it comes to telling the truth. And this is where courage comes into play. In addition to the fear of disappointing people or pushing

---

7. Brown, *The Gifts of Imperfection*, 39.

them away with the truths about who we really are, we can also be afraid that if we tell our stories truthfully, people won't like us anymore. This is what happened to Laurie who worked up the courage to tell her neighbor that she was a recovering alcoholic, only to have her neighbor say, "I'm not sure I'm comfortable with my kids playing at your house anymore." Laurie had worked hard to develop the courage to tell the truth to this neighbor about this part of her life. So, she responded by saying "but they've played here for two years, and I've been sober for twenty years. I'm not any different than I was ten minutes ago. Why are you?"

Shame is often referred to as "the master emotion." When we experience shame, it can paralyze us and force us to silence our stories. And if we all have shame, the good news is that we are all capable of developing what I call "shame resilience." Shame resilience is the ability to recognize shame, to move through it constructively, and to ultimately develop more courage, compassion, and connection. The first thing we need to understand about shame resilience is that the less we talk about shame, the more we have it.

Basically, shame needs three things to grow out of control in our lives: secrecy, silence and judgment. When something shaming happens and we keep it locked up, it festers and grows. It consumes us. What we need to do is to have the courage to share our experience with someone. Talk about it with someone. Why? Because shame happens between people, and it heals between people. If we can find someone with whom we can share our story, we need to tell it. Shame loses power when it is spoken. This is what happened to Sarah.

Sarah was a remarkable woman who was referred to me because of depression and anxiety. The owner of a successful interior design firm, she was on friendly terms with many very creative people. Yet she had come because of a deep loneliness and a long string of self-destructive behaviors and relationships with men. She was a large woman of great warmth and humor and had a wonderful laugh.

Born in Ireland of a socially prominent Catholic family, she was raised in a traditional home in which she had felt safe and protected. As a young girl, she attended Catholic schools and traveled with her family to many wonderful places. It had been a pleasant and comfortable life.

"When did all this change?" I asked her. Painfully, she told me about an evening when she had left her boarding school on an errand and had been raped at knife point. She had received very little honest support from her overwhelmed parents or her church, who dealt with her shame by covering it over with silence. Shortly afterwards, she had left Ireland and moved to the States to live with an aunt.

Sarah had never shared her story with anyone except her parents and her pastor at her church. They didn't know how to help her, and so she kept this secret to herself. Although this happened twenty-five years ago, the rape had left her deeply wounded, vulnerable and shamed. She became unable to set personal boundaries or take control of her life. She took whatever came her way and tried to make the most of it. She really didn't believe that she could change things. However, at work, she was powerful and very competent, making shrewd decisions and running a successful business in a highly competitive field.

For more than a year, we talked about her experience which opened many old wounds and allowed some healing to begin. It was a safe environment for her. Talking about what happened to her and the impact this experience had on her life, allowed her to explore some conclusions she had drawn about herself and about life. After several months of this, we began to examine how she lived her own life. For many years, she had spent her life without knowing how to grow emotionally or how to work through all these feelings. I told her that she had very little experience in knowing how to care for herself and I suggested she begin a practice to enable her to learn this. "Did I mean meditation?" she asked. "Not exactly," I said. "Buy a plant." She laughed her wonderful laugh and said she did not think she could keep a plant alive. But that was just the point. Although she was doubtful, she agreed to try.

Over the next several months, Sarah struggled to keep the plant alive. Her task was to pay attention to it every day, noticing its needs and responding to them. At first it was touch and go. Her plant suffered from overindulgence followed by periods of neglect, much like Sarah herself. "Listen, more carefully," I encouraged her. "If you really pay attention, it will show you what it needs."

Sarah's plant was tenacious. Despite some hard times, it would recover and continue to grow. Sarah began to admire its resilience and she began to see something of herself in it. She spoke to me about its strength and ability to continue to grow despite some difficulties. Gradually, she got better at recognizing its needs.

At about this time, Sarah began to consider making some changes to her life. The demands of her work were enormous, and she had very little time for herself. Building on a new trust in her own judgment and her ability to know what she needed, she sold her business and opened a design school. She had always wanted to do this but doubted herself and never had the courage to take the chance. Now, she was ready. Then, about this time, she met a good, kind man and began dating him. Over the next several months, as she moved into this new life and this new relationship, she no longer felt a need for our sessions.

A few years later, I received an invitation to her wedding. She and her husband are now settled in Virginia in their first home. Proudly, she showed me pictures. Her yard was enormous. When I commented on its beauty, she smiled, "I planted it myself."

Finally, it is important to understand that there is a difference between shame and guilt. This can best be understood as the difference between "I am bad" and "I did something bad."

Guilt means I did something bad. Shame means I am bad. Shame is about "who we are," and guilt is about "our behaviors." We feel guilty when we hold up something we've done or failed to do against the kind of person we want to be. It's an uncomfortable feeling, but one that can be helpful. Why? Because when we apologize for something we've done, make amends to others, or change a behavior that we don't feel good about, guilt is most often the motivator, not shame. Guilt can be just as powerful as shame, but its effect can often be positive while shame is often destructive. In addition, shame is much more likely to lead to destructive and hurtful behaviors than it is to be the solution. All of us want to feel worthy of love and belonging. But when we experience shame, we feel disconnected and desperate for worthiness. Then, we are more likely to engage in self-destructive behaviors and to even attack or try to shame others. In fact, shame is very much related to violence, aggression, depression, addiction, eating disorders and bullying. Children who use more shame self-talk (I am bad) versus guilt self-talk (I did something bad) struggle mightily with issues of self-worth and self-loathing. And using shame to parent, teaches children that they are not inherently worthy of love.

In John Steinbeck's splendid novel, *East of Eden,* there is a scene in which a son gives his father a present that he has selected with great care and for which he has sacrificed a great deal. The father spurns it. The reader understands that the father does this because he is an emotionally wounded person who has trouble seeing his son's better qualities and also has difficulty believing that he himself deserves a special present. But the boy, lacking the reader's prospective, doesn't understand. The message he gets is that he is not good enough, and that rejection will color the rest of his life.

There are a lot of people in the world like this boy and Susan and Sarah, walking around feeling like they are not good enough, feeling disappointed in who they are and not believing they deserve to be loved. There can also be something in ourselves that causes us to think less of ourselves every time we do something wrong. It may be the result of parents who expected too much of us, or maybe teachers or someone important to us, who took for granted what we did right and focused instead on everything we got wrong.

So often we feel we need to be perfect in order for us to love ourselves or for other people to love us and that somehow we forfeit that love if we ever fall short of perfection. There are few emotions more capable of leaving us feeling bad about ourselves than the conviction that we don't deserve to be loved. But God doesn't stop loving us every time we do something wrong, and neither should we stop loving ourselves and each other for being less than perfect.

Several years ago, the well known author, Rabbi Harold Kushner, wrote a book entitled *How Good Do We Have To Be?* In this work, Kushner emphasizes the fact that no one is perfect. Yet many people measure themselves and others against impossibly high standards. But the result is always the same—guilt, anger, depression, and disappointment. A healthier approach, Kushner maintains, is to learn how to put our human shortcomings into proper perspective. We need to learn how to accept ourselves and others even when we and they are less than perfect.[8] In my years as a psychotherapist, I have learned a number of things about perfectionism from my clients.

Perfectionism is found, in varying degrees, in many people. We twist ourselves into knots, doing things to gain the approval and love of others. It would be much healthier if we could let go of what people think and accept ourselves, warts and all.

The quest for perfection is exhausting. We need to be gentle and compassionate with ourselves, particularly when we make mistakes. We need to stop holding ourselves to ridiculously high standards in a quest to prove our worth to others. We are already enough. Compassion towards ourselves leads to compassion towards others.

---

8. Kushner, *How Good Do We Have To Be?*, 4.

Having the courage to let others see who we really are—to see the parts of ourselves that are not perfect, can be very healing. When we are our authentic selves, we end up connecting with others on a deeper level. Don't we love the company of people who are real and comfortable in their own skin?

One of my clients told me one time that she had always worked hard at being good enough. For her, it was the golden standard by which she decided what to read, what to wear, how to act, how to spend time, where to live, and even what to say. Even good enough was not really good enough for her. She said she had spent a lifetime trying to make herself perfect. When she came to see me, she was exhausted and depressed. What she needed was to simply understand that she was human. She had always feared that she would be "found out."

It's important to understand the difference between healthy striving and perfectionism. Perfectionism is not the same thing as striving to be your best. Perfectionism is *not* about healthy achievement and growth. Rather, it is the belief that if we look perfect, act perfect, and live perfectly, we can minimize or avoid the pain of blame, judgment, and shame. It's like a shield. Perfectionism is a twenty-ton shield that we lug around thinking it will protect us when, in fact, it's the thing that's really preventing us from taking flight.

Perfectionism is also not self-improvement. Perfectionism is, at its core, about trying to earn approval and acceptance. Most perfectionists were raised being praised for achievement and performance—grades, manners, rule-following, people-pleasing, appearance, sports, etc. Somewhere along the way, we adopt this dangerous and debilitating belief system. "I am what I accomplish and how well I accomplish it." *Please, Perform. Perfect.* Healthy striving is self-focused—*how can I improve?* Perfectionism is other-focused—*What will they think?* Children can learn early that they are loved for what they do and not simply for who they are. To a perfectionistic parent, for example, what you do never seems as good as what you might do if you just tried a little harder. The life of such children can become a constant striving to earn love. Of course, love is never earned. It is a grace that we give one another. Anything else is only approval. Often, perfectionists cannot tell the difference between love and approval.

Long before Tim went to medical school, he was trained to be a perfectionist by his father. As a child, when he brought home a ninety-eight on an exam, his father responded, "what happened to the other two points?"

Tim adored his dad, and his entire childhood was focused on the pursuit of the other two points. By the time he was in his twenties, he had become as much a perfectionist as his father was. It was no longer necessary for his father to ask him about those two points. Tim had taken that over for himself. It was many years before he found out that those two points don't matter. They are not the secret to living a life worth remembering. They don't make you lovable or whole.

Fortunately, life offers us many teachers. One of Tim's was his good friend, David, who was an artist. One day they were talking and Tim happened to mention that his driver's license was coming up for renewal and that he needed to take a written test on the traffic laws. The DMV had sent him a little booklet. Tim studied it for days. During those days while Tim was memorizing the meaning of the white curb and yellow curb, David would try to persuade him to join him for a walk or go to a party or go out to dinner. Tim told him he couldn't take the time. He had to study. In the end, Tim received 100 percent on the test. Feeling triumphant, he rushed into David's studio shouting his good news. David looked up from his painting with an expression of great kindness. "Why," he said, "would you want to do that?"

It was not the response that Tim had expected. Suddenly, he understood that he had sacrificed a great deal to get a hundred on a test that he had only needed to pass in order to drive. He had spent hours studying for it that he could have spent in much wiser ways. He had learned many things that he did not even want to know! But Tim really felt as if he had no choice. If his father could not approve of him with anything less than 100 percent, he could not approve of himself with less than 100 percent either. Even on a written driving test.

However, this entire experience was not really about driving. It was not even about grades. It was about needing to deserve love. Fortunately, his friend David did not play by these rules. He didn't even know the game.

How freeing it is to know that we don't need to be perfect to be loved. That we don't need to get 100 percent on so many dimensions of life. Moreover, we can truly love others because they are not perfect either. In other words, it's ok to be human. And maybe this is the more difficult challenge. Maybe this actually requires more courage. Appreciating our own humanness and the humanness of others, we realize that each of us is a work in progress. Each of us is like an unfinished symphony. Perhaps one word in our English language that we probably don't use very often is the word *yet*.

But it is very important in understanding who we are. Maybe it would be most accurate to add the word *yet* to all our assessments of ourselves and each other. Bill has not learned compassion . . . *yet*. I have not developed courage . . . *yet*. I am not as kind as I would like to be . . . *yet*. It changes everything. It allows us to become less perfectionistic, less critical, less judgmental about life itself. If life truly is a journey, a process, then all judgments are provisional. We can't judge something until it is finished—even ourselves. Each of us is a work in progress. We are not finished . . . *yet*. No one has won or lost until the race is over.

Perfectionistic people can be profoundly judgmental about most things. What is lacking always seems so clear to them. However, this way of judging life colors a person's reactions to themselves and those around them. As a person struggles to free themselves from this way of seeing life, it allows them to grow into a place where we see the need for one another which then allows us to join together in becoming more whole.

Research shows that perfectionism actually hampers success. In fact, it's often the path to depression, anxiety, addiction, and life paralysis. *Life paralysis* refers to all of the opportunities we miss because we're too afraid to put anything out in the world that could possibly be imperfect. It's also all of the dreams that we don't follow because of our deep fear of failing, making mistakes, and disappointing others. It's terrifying to risk when you're a perfectionist. Your self-worth is on the line.

In reality, perfectionism is a self-destructive and addictive belief system that fuels this primary thought: "If I look perfect, live perfectly, and do everything perfectly, I can avoid or immunize the painful feelings of shame, judgment, and blame. Therefore, perfectionism is more about *perception*—we want to be perceived as perfect. However, this is unattainable—there is no way to control perception, regardless of how much time and energy we spend trying.

Finally, perfectionism is addictive because when we invariably do experience shame, judgment, and blame, we often believe it's because we weren't perfect enough. So, rather than questioning the faulty logic of perfectionism, we become even more entrenched in our quest to live, look, and do everything just right.

In order to overcome perfectionism, we need the courage to practice self-compassion. When we become more loving and compassionate with ourselves, we can embrace our imperfections. Interestingly enough, it is in the process of embracing our imperfections that we find our truest gifts: courage, love, and connection.

Christopher Germer once wrote that "a moment of self-compassion can change your entire day. A string of such moments can change the course of your life."[9] The word compassion is derived from the Latin words *pati* and *cum*, meaning "to suffer with." But how many of us really apply this term to ourselves? Most of the time, we think of being more compassionate toward others. How helpful it would be if we could apply it to ourselves because the heart of compassion is really acceptance. The better we are at accepting ourselves and others, the more compassionate we become. This is why self-compassion can be extremely helpful in accepting and loving ourselves. It allows us to integrate those parts of ourselves that we struggle with in a positive way so that we can grow into the person we want to be. And, in order to develop this kind of self-compassion, we need two things: 1) self-kindness, and 2) emotional balance. Self-kindness means being warm and understanding toward ourselves when we fail or feel inadequate, rather than ignoring our faults or beating ourselves up with self-criticism. Emotional balance recognizes that suffering and feelings of personal inadequacies are part of our shared human experience. It's something we all go through rather than something that happens to "me" alone. It also means taking a balanced approach to negative emotions so that these kinds of feelings are neither suppressed nor exaggerated. Emotional balance requires that we not "overly-identify" with thoughts and feelings, so that we are caught up and swept away by negativity. I think these ideas are key for those of us who struggle with being perfect and getting down on ourselves.

In my counseling practice, I have seen that people who are compassionate toward themselves often possess two qualities: 1) they speak about their imperfections in a tender and honest way, and without shame or fear. 2) They are slow to judge themselves and others. They appear to operate from a place that says, "we are all human and doing the best we can."

Most of us are trying to live authentic lives and become the person God wants us to be. Deep down, we want to stop pretending and love and accept ourselves "warts and all." There is a line from Leonard Cohen's song "Anthem" that serves as a reminder to me when I get into that place where I'm trying to control everything and make it perfect. The line is, "there is

---

9. Germer, *The Mindful Path to Self-Compassion. See also:* https://www.goodreads.com/author/quotes.christophergermer.

a crack in everything. That's how the light gets in."[10] So many of us run around trying to spackle all the cracks, trying to make everything look just right. This line can help us remember the beauty of the cracks—like the messy house, the imperfect manuscript, and the jeans that are too tight. It reminds us that our imperfections and shortcomings are not inadequacies. They are simply reminders that we are all in this together. Imperfectly, but together.

James Hollis, in his book *Living an Examined Life*, talks about how each of us is part of a great mosaic.

> Each of us has a gift, the essential gift of being who we are, with all the flaws, shortcomings, mistakes, and fears of which we are all so aware. . . . We are all here to be ourselves. . . . And our gift to the great mosaic of the world is our uniqueness. Each of us has something to bring to the mosaic of time that is unfolding in and through us whether we are aware of it or not.[11]

Soren Kierkegaard said "don't forget to love yourself."[12] Sometimes, it helps to wake up in the morning and tell ourselves, "today, I'm going to believe that showing up is enough."

C. The Courage to Accept and Love People Who are Different from Us

As an assistant professor of spirituality in a graduate school of theology program, I have had the privilege of attending graduation ceremonies. One year, I was at a commencement when Bob received his diploma. Bob was well known and liked at our school. He was an openly gay man and was a respected minister in the Metropolitan Community Church. Comfortable with his orientation, he founded the Gay and Lesbian Center on campus and worked very well with many organizations at the college.

On graduation day, I remember seeing his father for the first time. He wore dark jeans and a black leather biker jacket with a bandana that covered his forehead. He was very muscular and looked like he could have been a bouncer at the local bar. As I watched him and his wife file into their reserved seats, I couldn't help but wonder what it must have been like for this gay man to grow up in this family.

---

10. https://genius.com/leonardcohen.
11. Hollis, *Living an Examined Life*, in *Well for the Journey*, May 7, 2018.
12 https://www.brainyquote.com/lists/authors/top_10_soren_kierkegaard_quotes.

The ceremony proceeded without incident. Names were read and diplomas were distributed as the graduates filed across the stage. The time came for Bob's row to rise and approach the platform. Bob ascended the stairs and as the dean called his name, his dad rose from his chair with his fist outstretched and shouted, "that's my boy!"

You could almost hear the audience gasp as they reacted to Bob's father's exclamation.

Clearly, this was a proud father who genuinely loved his son. But what those in attendance that day didn't know was the interior struggle that his father had gone through to come to a point where he could accept his son for who he was. In the beginning, the reality of Bob being gay was immensely difficult for this "biker dad" to accept. For months, he struggled to accept this. Finally, with the help of a therapist, he came to understand that Bob's sexuality was only a part of who he was as a person.

As I reflected back on that day, I remembered what happened at the baptism of Jesus when a voice came from heaven saying, "you are my son, my beloved, in whom I take great delight" (Mark 1: 11). In the eyes of the Father that Jesus knew, we are all sons and daughters of the divine. Each of us is beloved. What a wonderful thought. Our God "delights" in us. No matter who we are, or what our beliefs are, we are all held in the sacred radiance that delights in our beauty and giftedness. God gazes upon each of us and is both moved when we suffer and delighted when we flourish. Before the face of our anguish, God's eyes are moist. In the radiance of our beauty, God beams with boundless pride. This is what Bob's father felt when he shouted, "that's my boy!" That's my beloved. And in him, I am so delighted.

It is always challenging to accept people for who they are rather than who we want them to be. This is especially true if the way in which they are different is important to us. For example, if we don't like something a person is doing but the issue is not very important to us, then eventually it will become easier to accept if we can't change it. However, if the issue is something that is very important to us, then the struggle to accept it becomes all the more difficult. This is why the Serenity Prayer has become more meaningful to me as I have gotten older. "Lord, grant me the serenity to accept the things in life I can't change, to change the things I can, and the wisdom to know the difference."

Everyone wants to be seen and accepted for who they are. In my experience as a psychotherapist, this is generally easy to do for most of us if we like the person, if our beliefs are relatively similar, or if our opinions are pretty much the same. But our real challenge is to accept and love people who are sometimes very different from us. To try and understand something from someone else's point of view, to walk in someone else's shoes is extremely challenging. And this is where courage comes in. Maybe we associate with some people who believe differently than we do on social issues, on political issues, about the LGBT community, about peace and justice issues, on church and religious issues, etc. Do we just write them off because they don't agree with our ideas and opinions? This would certainly not be the Christian response. But it can take courage to accept them for their beliefs and to stand up for our own beliefs as we talk with them about particular topics. Differences among us, don't have to divide us.

Through the years, Dorothy Day has been a model as a person who loved, lived with, and dedicated her life to serving the poor and people who were very different from her. Psychiatrist, teacher, and author Robert Coles has written a moving account of the day in 1952 when, as a young and discouraged medical student, he met Dorothy. He found himself one afternoon at the Catholic Worker soup kitchen, having made an earlier decision to engage in some useful volunteer work. This is the story of his first encounter with Dorothy.

> She was sitting at a table, talking with a woman who was, I quickly realized, quite drunk, yet determined to carry on a conversation. ... The woman to whom Dorothy Day was talking ... had a large purple birthmark along the right side of her forehead. She kept touching it as she uttered one exclamatory remark after another, none of which seemed to get the slightest rise from the person sitting opposite her.
>
> I found myself increasingly confused by what seemed to be an interminable essentially absurd exchange taking place between two middle-aged women. When would it end—the alcoholic ranting and the silent nodding, occasionally interrupted by a brief question, which only served, maddeningly, to wind up the already over-talkative one rather than wind her down? Finally, silence fell upon the room. She got up and came over to me. She said, 'Are you waiting to talk to one of us?'
>
> *One of us:* with those three words she had cut through layers of self-importance, a life-time of bourgeois privilege, and scraped the hard bone of pride.... With those three words, she had indirectly

Courage and our Personalities

told me what the Catholic Worker Movement is all about and what she herself was like.[13]

During the years he knew her, Coles would learn many things from Dorothy Day, but this particular lesson would serve as a basis for everything else. He never forgot how she treated this person who was very different from her. Dorothy's use of the words "one of us" placed the ranting, alcoholic woman on a par with herself, and, for that moment at least, clothed her with respect. That afternoon in the Catholic Worker house, Dorothy and her companion were, to use a phrase by psychiatrist Gerald May, two notes in the human symphony—one harmonious and one discordant, one sweet and one harsh, but both part of the same song. Dorothy was possessed by a connection of the presence of Christ in everyone. It was this certainty of his radiant love alive in every person that compelled her to live in service of that love, regardless of how unlikely or unattractive a vessel she might find it.

We seem to live in an age today when this idea of reverence and respect has lost much of its importance in life, especially for people who are different from us. When we look around us, there seems to be so much irreverence and disrespect. The way we often treat one another is an indication of that. But it is such an important dimension of life. It colors so much of how we go about living each day.

So, what does it mean to be reverent and respectful? What does it mean to love and accept people who are very different from us? While this is certainly not an exhaustive list, I would say it means some of the following things.

First of all, I think it has a lot to do with the way Dorothy treated that lady who was drunk. She was able to look beyond her drinking problem and saw her being a child of God and possessing the presence of Christ. Then, because of this, she was willing to spend time with her and in the process gave her dignity. Having reverence and respect for others, enables us to have a basic stance in life where we try to see the presence of Christ in everyone. This, then, will allow us to treat each person with dignity and respect.

Secondly, I think having reverence and respect means basically trying to live the Golden Rule which encourages us to always treat others as we would like to be treated, even if they are different from us. This will

---

13. Coles, *Dorothy Day*, xviii.

encourage us to never look down on anyone, never think ourselves better than anyone because very often, we don't know their story.

Thirdly, having reverence and respect for others means that we don't use people for our own pleasure or gain. We don't use people to get ahead in life or to gain something for ourselves. With this kind of outlook, we can choose to treat others with kindness and compassion. This way of living allows us to realize that we are not here to dominate anyone or anything but rather to do our part to make the world a more gentle place.

Finally, maybe one of the greatest blessings we can offer others is the belief we have in their struggle for freedom—the courage to support and accompany them as they determine for themselves the strength that will become the foundation of their lives. As a psychotherapist, I have had the opportunity and privilege to do this with some of my clients through the years. To affirm their person as they strive to discover for themselves who they are and what is important to them in life. I think it is especially important to believe in someone at a time when they cannot yet believe in themselves. Then your belief will become their lifeline. As one gay man told me, "you have seen me and I am grateful." Sometimes, simply being accepted as you are and cared about by another can affect a person in very profound ways.

D. The Courage to Face into Our Fears

For over twenty years, we lived in Maryland near the Chesapeake Bay Bridge. It is a very long suspension bridge that crosses a very large part of the Chesapeake Bay. Over the years, I have had a number of clients who were afraid to drive across the bridge. The problem was made worse due to the fact that if you didn't drive across the bridge to get to the other side, it was about a three hour drive to go around a different way. For some of my clients, the fear was so great that they were almost paralyzed. If the fear was so strong and the person was alone, the person could actually pay a driver to take them across to the other side.

If you are not afraid to drive across bridges, it can be difficult to understand how anyone can be so afraid of doing this. And—how much courage it takes for the person to be able to accomplish this. With several of my clients, it was a slow process but one that was worth working on because our fears have a tendency to build on each other. Fear within a person can be like a cancer that begins with one thing and then grows into other areas of our lives. That is why it is so important to "face into our fears."

Each of us can be afraid of things in our own way. Fear is an honest human emotion. We don't have to apologize for being afraid. But it is very important for each of us to learn how to deal with our fears. And that takes courage. How we do that can be very different.

One of my clients had been locked in a web of fear for years when she came to see me. After listening to Deborah's fears and trying various strategies for over six months with minimal success, I decided to try a new approach to help her cope with her fears. One day, I told her that for the next four weeks she was simply not allowed to be afraid. She looked at me with confusion, unable to imagine what I meant. Carefully, I explained to her that I had observed that her first reaction to just about everything was fear and that when people had one reaction to everything, that reaction became suspect. In short, I didn't believe that all her fear was true.

Abruptly, she became angry, telling me that I was not very compassionate and indeed did not understand her. "No," I said, "I believe that after all these months, I do understand you very well. This fear that has so little to do with who you truly are has gotten in the way of your growth." After she had calmed down, she asked again what it was that I was suggesting that she do. She reminded me again that she experienced fear many times every day. "I know," I told her, "and I am just proposing an experiment which will require a great deal of courage on your part." I suggested that whenever she felt fear that she think of it as only her first response to whatever was happening. The most familiar response, as it were. But then I encouraged her to look for her second response and follow that. "Ask yourself," 'if I was not afraid, if I were not allowed to be afraid, how would I respond to what is happening?'" She was reluctant, but she agreed to try.

At first, Deborah had been discouraged to notice how many times she experienced fear every day. This exercise made her acutely aware of this. But gradually, she was surprised to find that often she could step beyond her initial stab of fear with some ease, and try not to pay attention to it. It was then that she found she had a wide variety of different reactions to the events in her life. It had never occurred to her to challenge her fears in this way before.

After a few months, she even began to wonder whether she, herself, was afraid. For the first time, she questioned if the fear that had been her life's constant companion was just like a habit, a knee-jerk response to life that she had learned years ago. Over the next few months, whenever she felt fear, she would stop and ask herself if it were true, looking closely to see if she really was afraid. Surprisingly, she often discovered she was not.

Over time, Deborah found that she also was not afraid to try when she was not sure she could succeed, not afraid to speak out in defense of her values, not afraid to confront an angry person, not afraid to introduce herself to someone and help them, and not afraid to submit her work to others. Her mother had been afraid of all these things. All of this took a great deal of courage on her part but Deborah had come to discover that facing into her fears gave her a new sense of freedom and enabled her to grow as a person.

As we continued to work with her fears, Deborah remembered that staying safe had been the most important thing in her mothers's life. She came to understand that she had internalized this way of thinking and living. But she also came to realize that staying safe was not the way she wanted to live her life. Her mother had lived a very narrow and unhappy life, mostly because of her fears. At the end of our sessions, Deborah told me that "if you carry someone's fear and live by someone else's values, you may find that you have lived their lives rather than your own."

Trying to face into our fears requires a lot of courage. Many of us are more inclined to run away from them or hide from them or keep ourselves so distracted that they don't dominate our lives. However, very often, in my experience, if we do this, it will only make them worse. Facing into a fear and tackling it head on begins a process in ourselves of handling it in a constructive way. It builds our confidence in our ability to deal with whatever we have to deal with in life. It also helps us learn to trust ourselves and to believe that we are capable of making good, healthy decisions.

It is interesting to see in the Gospels that the apostles were often anxious and afraid. Many times, their fear was caused by the unknown. It seems as though Jesus was constantly trying to encourage them to trust Him and not to worry or be afraid. One time, when Jesus got into a boat, followed by his disciples, a storm broke out over the lake. Matthew says that the storm was so violent that the waves were breaking over the boat. But Jesus was asleep. So, they went to Him and woke Him saying, "save us Lord, we are going down!" And He said to them, "why are you so frightened, you men of little faith?" And with that He stood up and rebuked the winds and the sea and all was calm again" (Matt 8: 23-27). At another time, Jesus told his disciples not to worry about your life and what you are to eat, nor about your body and how you are to clothe it. "Look at the birds," He said. "They do not sow or reap or gather into barns; yet your heavenly Father feeds them. Are you not worth much more than they are? Can any of you, for all your worrying, add one single cubit to his span of life? . . . So do not worry about tomorrow. Tomorrow will take care of itself. Each day has enough trouble of its own" (Matt 6: 25–34). And similarly, in John's Gospel, Jesus tells his disciples: "do not let your hearts be troubled, or afraid" (Jn 14: 27).

Even Jesus had to face into his own fears. He set Jerusalem as his destination, knowing that He would be crucified there. Can we ever begin to imagine the courage it would take to go to a town where we know we would be killed? He allowed Himself to face into his fear, and did not let the fear control him. And in the garden of Gethsemane, his anguish was so intense that he sweated blood.

I think that the words of Jesus can help each of us face into our fears, so that they don't dominate our lives. "Do not be afraid. It is I." "Do not let your hearts be troubled." If we can allow his words to penetrate our hearts, we will know that He is with us to calm our fears. If we can trust in the Lord to always be with us, we can surrender our fears to Him. Surrender is like letting go and letting God. It is believing that He is always with us and stronger than our fears.

In my experience, maybe more than any single thing, fear is the stumbling block to living life gratefully. Perhaps it is only the things we fear that we wish to control. But this can be exhausting. No one can serve life and grow in a life of gratitude if they are afraid of life. Life is a process. Deborah had worked hard to understand her fears and become free of them. In the beginning, it required more courage than she thought she ever possessed. In the end, she felt that she had a new lease on life—a new inner freedom to be who she truly was. Sometimes, it takes a long time to face into our fears and become free. But that doesn't matter. It may be the most worthwhile way to spend our time.

E. The Courage to Face Our Limitations

Susan is blind. She has been this way for many years and often wonders what it would be like to see again. Having survived a head injury over twenty years ago, she says she often encounters two religious reactions to her disability: saint or sinner. On the one hand, friends and strangers alike say: "It is so amazing how you do all the things you do, even though you are blind. I could never do what you do if I were disabled like that." Sometimes, these comments are followed by, "well, everything happens for a reason; God must have a special plan for you." On the other hand, Susan has also been told with equal fervor that disability is a result of sin or a lack of faith, which if strong enough, would surely bring about physical healing.

For Susan, being blind has caused her much heartache and anguish which she has tried to learn to deal with. It has certainly been challenging to learn how to accept and live with this major limitation. As a blind woman, she confronts these limitations that are big and small on a daily basis. For example, she told me that she is obviously limited in her ability to drive a car, read a bedtime story to her son, match her socks, navigate through unfamiliar spaces without the risk of crashing into an obstacle, find her friend in a crowd, distinguish between a can of soup and a can of black beans, or catch a baseball. The list could go on and on. While none of these activities are essential to living, her inability to conduct them with the ease afforded to most people constantly reminds her of her real, concrete limitations in life.

Growing up the daughter of a Mennonite minister in a tight-knit, relatively insular Protestant denomination, Susan attended Mennonite schools and was surrounded by Mennonite friends. After much personal, religious, and academic reflection, she earned a Ph.D. in religious studies, and she now teaches world religions at a liberal arts women's college. Her husband is an Episcopal priest.

I remember when I was in college, I had a very interesting discussion with my roommate about whether it was more difficult to be blind or deaf. I always thought blindness was more difficult because it was more limiting in life than deafness. But my roommate thought deafness was more limiting. After discussing these ideas for awhile, I remember my roommate saying, "can you imagine the courage, the strength it would take for a person to live with either of these limitations? When I first met Susan, all of this came back to me. Imagine the courage it would take to face the realities of each day if you were blind. This is one of the hidden faces of courage that some people have to live with each and every day. The courage and strength that Susan needed to constantly ask all kinds of people to help her do so many things in life. The courage to face the frustrations of each day, the courage to face the reality of each day without being able to see a single thing, and to do this without being angry and resentful.

Courage and our Personalities

Susan has been blind now for over twenty years. After the accident, she went through several years in which she was terribly angry and depressed. This is when I began seeing her on a regular basis. Gradually, with the help of her parents, siblings, and several good friends, she began to accept her situation. Eventually, she decided to work with other blind people in order to help them cope with their situation. What really helped her and was a turning point in her life was a book that one of her professors in her doctoral program recommended. The book was entitled *Disability and Christian Theology: Embodied Limits and Constructive Possibilities* by Deborah Beth Creamer. It articulated a new model for thinking about limitations and disabilities. It is simply called the "limits model," and this model highlights the fact that human limits need not, and perhaps should not, be seen as negative or as something that cannot be done, and instead claims that limits are an important part of being human.

This limits model says that we all share in the experience of limitation in one form or another. It suggests that it is in and through our experiences of limitation that we understand what it means to be human. From the perspective of the limits model, blindness is simply one form of human limitation and can give all of us a unique perspective and insight into what it means to live with limitations. Maybe more importantly, the limits model says that we are all limited in some way and we need to rely on one another precisely because of our limitations. It also helps us as Christians to view the church as a community of wounded people sharing the experience of limitation where God is present in the midst of vulnerability, dependency, and limitations. Susan's blindness and the limits model offer us the opportunity to reflect on our own limitations. What do they teach us about what it means to be human? What do they teach us about living with courage? What do our limitations teach us about living in community with other people who are also limited? What do they teach us about being a child of God? Finally, what do they teach us about letting go of the myths of self-sufficiency, individualism, and independence? Susan's struggle to cope with her limitation offers each of us the opportunity to integrate our limitations into our own efforts to grow in life.

In chapter ten of Mark's Gospel, we read about Bartimaeus, a blind beggar.

> As he left Jericho with his disciples and a large crowd, Bartimaeus, a blind beggar, was sitting at the side of the road. When he heard that it was Jesus of Nazareth, he began to shout and to say, 'Son

of David, Jesus, have pity on me.' And many of them scolded him and told him to keep quiet, but he only shouted all the louder, 'Son of David, have pity on me.' Jesus stopped and said, 'call him here.' So they called to the blind man. 'Courage,' they said 'get up; he is calling you.' So throwing off his cloak, he jumped up and went to Jesus. Then Jesus spoke. 'What do you want me to do for you?' 'Rabboni,' the blind man said to him 'Master, let me see again.' Jesus said to him, 'Go; your faith has saved you.' And immediately his sight returned and he followed him along the road (Mark 10: 46–52).

We may not be physically blind like Susan or Bartimaeus, but we can be blind in so many other ways. What about the blindness we have into our own behavior? The reasons why we do the things we do? What about our blindness to our envy or jealousy? Or the blindness of how we manipulate people and situations to our own advantage? What about our blindness to other people in need? How we can technically "see" the poor and homeless but tend to walk right by them? Or, what about our blindness to social justice and peace issues? Physical blindness is not the only way we don't "see" things. But just as it takes a lot of courage each day for Susan to face her limitations, so, in the same way, it takes a lot of courage for each of us to face our blindness, our own ways of not completely "seeing."

Bartimaeus asked Jesus to cure his physical blindness. Susan also prayed for this kind of healing. Fortunately, most of us don't have to struggle with this kind of physical limitation but we still need the Lord to heal each of the ways that we can be blind. Maybe, like Bartimaeus, our prayer can be "Master, let me see again."

F. The Courage To Forgive

Forgiveness requires a lot of courage. It is one of those hidden faces of courage that all of us struggle with. It is so difficult because it involves so many dimensions of our humanness. Sometimes, I become impatient with people who seem to think it is so easy. That certainly has not been my experience or the reality of many of my clients over the years. It is difficult because all of us have been hurt in life and these wounds often cause emotional turmoil which takes time to work through. That is why forgiveness usually involves a process. We have to work our way through many emotions in order to come to a point where we can truly forgive rather than simply excuse.

Courage and our Personalities

Everett Worthington put it very well in his book *Forgiving and Reconciling* when he said, "the way of forgiveness is hard. Forgiveness isn't for wimps."[14]

Close to the end of Morrie Schwartz's life, author Mitch Album in *Tuesdays with Morrie,* asked him about the idea of forgiveness. Morrie seemed eager to share his thoughts on this topic.

> Forgive yourself before you die. Then forgive others. There is no point in keeping vengeance or stubbornness. These things I so regret in my life. Vanity. Why do we do the things we do?
>
> Mitch wondered if Morrie had any need to say I'm sorry to anyone before he died. Do you see that sculpture? Morrie asked, pointing to the figure on a shelf against the wall of his office. Cast in bronze, it was the face of a man in his early forties, wearing a necktie, a tuft of hair falling across his forehead. That's me, Morrie said. A friend of mine, sculpted that maybe thirty years ago. His name was Norman. We used to spend so much time together. We went swimming. We took rides to New York. He had me over to his house in Cambridge, and he sculpted that bust of me down in his basement. It took several weeks to do, but he really wanted to get it right.[15]

Mitch studied the face. Since Morrie was in the final stage of his life, suffering from ALS, he thought how strange it was to see a three-dimensional Morrie, so healthy, so young. Even in bronze, Morrie seemed to have a whimsical look about him.

> Well, here's the sad part of the story, Morrie said. Norman and his wife moved away to Chicago. A little while later, my wife, Charlotte, had to have a pretty serious operation. Norman and his wife never got in touch with us. I knew they knew about it. Charlotte and I were very hurt because they never called to see how she was. So we dropped the relationship. Over the years, I met Norman a few times and he always tried to reconcile, but I didn't accept it. I wasn't satisfied with his explanation. I was prideful. I shrugged him off. A few years ago he died of cancer. I feel so sad. I never got to see him. I never got to forgive. It pains me now so much.[16]

Morrie went on to say that

> It's not just other people we need to forgive. We also need to forgive ourselves. Ourselves, Mitch said. Yes. For all the things we didn't

---

14. Worthington, *Forgiving and Reconciling,* 15.
15. Albom, *Tuesdays with Morrie,* 164–65.
16. Ibid., 165–66.

do. All the things we should have done. You can't get stuck on the regrets of what should have happened. That doesn't help you when you get to where I am. I always wished I had done more with my work. I wished I had written more books. I used to beat myself up over it. Now I see that never did any good. Make peace. You need to make peace with yourself and everyone around you. Forgive yourself. Forgive others. Don't wait, Mitch. Not everyone gets the time I'm getting. Not everyone is as lucky. I mourn my dwindling time, but I cherish the chance it gives me to make things right.[17]

Even a quick reading of the Gospels, indicates how important this topic was for Jesus. As early as chapter two in Mark's Gospel, Jesus cures the paralytic and begins a discussion with the scribes by saying, "my child, your sins are forgiven." Then He cures the man (Mark 2: 1–12). In Matthew, chapter five, Jesus tells his disciples that if your brother has something against you, leave your offering there before the altar, then go and be reconciled with your brother first (Matt 5: 24). In chapter six of Matthew's Gospel, He teaches us the Our Father. We are told in Luke 6: 36–37, to "be compassionate as your Father is compassionate. Do not judge . . . do not condemn . . . grant pardon." In Luke's Gospel, a woman who was known to be a sinner in the town, came to Simon's house to meet Jesus with her alabaster jar of ointment. She waited behind Him at his feet, weeping, and as her tears fell on his feet, she wiped them away with her hair. Then she kissed his feet and anointed them with her ointment. Jesus said to her, "your sins are forgiven" (Luke 7: 36–50). Using a parable in Matthew's Gospel, we learn the story of the unforgiving debtor and how we are supposed to forgive others their debts because our debts have been forgiven (Matt 18: 23–35). And certainly, one of the best examples of forgiveness that so many of us know is the story of the Prodigal Son where we are invited to be like the father who forgave both of his sons (Luke 15: 11–32). One final example I would like to mention which shows the incredible love that Jesus has for us are his words from the cross as He was dying, "Father forgive them, they do not know what they are doing" (Luke 23: 34). Even as He was dying on the cross, He continued to emphasize the importance of forgiveness.

Over and over again, I have seen in my work as a psychotherapist, the importance of forgiveness and the tremendous courage it takes to truly forgive someone. My clients have taught me this by sharing their lives with me.

I have learned from my clients that forgiveness is a healing of our own hearts. It removes the anger, bitterness, and the desire for revenge that

---

17. Ibid., 166–67.

we can experience when we have been hurt by someone. Elizabeth was a woman in her fifties when she first came to see me. At first, she described her life as being out of control. She felt impatient and angry most of the time and this was beginning to seriously affect her relationships at home as well as her job. For almost no reason at all, she said that she would snap at someone. This was especially true with her husband. She often knew that she was over reacting to someone or some situation but she couldn't seem to control herself. After several weeks of letting her speak and getting to know her better, she shared with me that she had been sexually abused by her brother when she was a young girl. She had never shared this with anyone except her husband. Since he didn't know how to help her, he encouraged her to find someone to talk to about this. For the next several months, we talked about this abuse issue and what it had done to her emotionally. She came to understand that much of her anger was caused by what her brother had done to her. Gradually, she gained more and more insight into what was motivating her angry behavior. Slowly, some of her anger began to dissipate. One day, I asked her what she would like to do about her brother. She said she would like to confront him about this personally but she was extremely hesitant because she did not know if he would admit to it or what his reaction would be like. Essentially, she was afraid to do this. I told her that I would be willing to be there with her if that would help. After discussing the pros and cons of this approach, she agreed. She asked him to come to a session and during this meeting she had a chance to confront him about what happened. She told him how angry she was at him and what this abuse had done to her. She described how much it had hurt her and affected her personality through the years.

After listening to her, the brother denied everything, saying that he couldn't remember doing anything like this to her. His response had clearly not been what Elizabeth had hoped for. However, it took a tremendous amount of inner courage and strength for her to take the initiative and talk with him about this abuse. Although she couldn't control his response concerning the abuse, it began a process in her where she could begin to let go of the anger, bitterness, and desire for revenge that had plagued her for years. Gradually, as she gained more insight and understood herself better, she began to work on her ultimate desire to forgive him. She came to understand that she could do this whether her brother wanted forgiveness or not.

Elizabeth's story is a good example of forgiveness on two levels. First, it was her effort to understand what this abuse had done to her through the years, begin to make some changes in her life, and work her way toward wanting to forgive her brother. But on another level, it is also an example of how Elizabeth could forgive someone who never asked for it or saw the need for it.

I have come to understand that our deepest desire is that the forgiveness we offer will be received. This mutuality between giving and receiving forgiveness is what creates peace and harmony. But if our condition for offering forgiveness is that it will be received, we might seldom forgive. This is because forgiveness is first and foremost an inner movement. It is an act that removes anger, bitterness, and the desire for revenge from our hearts and helps us to reclaim our human dignity. We can't force those we want to forgive into accepting our forgiveness. They might not be able or willing to do so. Like Elizabeth's brother, they might not even know or feel that they have wounded us.

In the final analysis, the only people we can really change are ourselves. What Elizabeth came to discover is that forgiving others is first and foremost a healing of our own hearts.

To forgive another person from the heart is really an act of liberation. We set that person free from the negative bonds that exist between us. We say, "I no longer hold your offense against you." But there is more. Maybe more importantly, we also free ourselves from the burden of being the *offended one*. As long as we do not forgive those who have wounded us, we continually carry them with us or, worse, pull them as a heavy load. The great temptation is to cling in anger to our enemies or those who have hurt us, and then define ourselves as being offended and wounded by them. Forgiveness, therefore, liberates not only the other person but also ourselves. It is the way to the inner freedom of the children of God.

The Challenge of Forgiving Ourselves

Maybe even more difficult to do and something that requires even more courage is forgiving ourselves. Carl Jung once said that the most difficult enemy we must face and forgive is the enemy within. Jung believed that we ourselves are in need of the kindness, compassion, and forgiveness that we may offer willingly to others.

Courage and our Personalities

In my counseling practice, I have seen many good, loving, and kind people who find it difficult to forgive themselves. Many them treat themselves with a depth of judgment and disgust that is completely at odds with their treatment of others.

Joe was a very good man who was down on himself for what I viewed as part of his humanness. As I listened to how he berated himself, I asked him, "Joe, if someone came to you and confessed to this same issue, would you tell them that you thought they were worthless and disgusting?" Joe said that he would never say these kinds of things to another person. Then I told him that it seemed to me that he believed his sins were worse than everyone else's, and that he was unworthy of the compassion he so willingly gave to others. "Are you really that awful, Joe?" "Apparently so," was his response.

Many of these people insist they know they are forgiven by God. The challenge is for them to accept this forgiveness and then to forgive themselves. For some people, this is easier said than done! If we haven't forgiven ourselves, we may prevent whatever light we have within us to shine and thereby not becoming all that God intends us to be. In his book, *Living Buddha, Living Christ,* writer Thich Nhat Hanh says that our capacity to make peace with another person in the world depends very much on our capacity to make peace with ourselves.[18] Similarly, Henri Nouwen wrote in *The Road to Daybreak: A Spiritual Journey,* that if I could fully accept the fact that I am forgiven and do not have to live in guilt or shame, I will truly be free.[19]

When I forgive, my message is this: "I see who you are, not what you have done. Now go and be yourself. Become all you are meant to be. Let your light shine." As with most elements of the spiritual journey, that cleansing freedom must start from within if we hope to give it to others.

Finally, sometimes we might need to find the courage to forgive an entire group of people or an organization so that we can be free. For example, this is so true for people who have been hurt and wounded by the actions of some in the catholic church. It might also be true for people who have been treated unfairly or unjustly by some organization.

This was certainly true for Dan. One day he told me about an experience that had been extremely painful for him. Dan said that he had been a

---

[18]. Hanh, *Living Buddha, Living Christ.* See also https:/www.goodreads.com/work/quotes 996684-livingbuddha-livingChrist.

[19]. Nouwen, *The Road to Daybreak: A Spiritual Journey.* See also https://www.goodreads.com/book/show/837601.The_Road_to_Daybreak.

member of a religious community for many years. During this time, he had formed may friendships with the members of his community. Certainly, in one sense, he felt they were all his brothers. Over time, several became good friends who shared life deeply. After approximately fifteen years, Dan said he began to become very depressed. He decided to go to counseling to help sort out the issues he was struggling with. After much prayer and soul searching, Dan decided to leave the community. It was the most difficult decision he ever had to make in his life. And it required a tremendous amount of courage. Dan went on to say that he realized his decision would change the nature of his friendships with his brothers in the community. He just didn't realize how much. Dan said he planned to stay in touch with his good friends in the community, but soon realized they didn't want that. After several attempts were made to continue his friendships, it gradually became clear that his efforts were not reciprocal. Even his best friend didn't want to stay in touch. He said he had struggled so much just to make this decision and felt devastated when his friends in the community didn't want to remain friends.

In order for Dan to find healing, he needed to find the courage to not only forgive his friends in the community but the community itself. This was so difficult for him because of the many years of service he had given to the community. As he struggled to find this kind of forgiveness, he went on to tell me that his efforts to forgive the community were helped when he received a call one day unexpectedly from his best friend in the community saying that he wanted to come and see Dan. Of course, Dan agreed and so his friend came to his home and apologized for the way that he, and the entire community had treated him over the years. Although the friendship never returned to the way it was in the community, Dan nevertheless felt this was a great grace for him in his life. It was clearly a healing moment and one that was extremely instrumental in Dan being able to find the courage to forgive the community.

G. The Courage To Grieve

It takes courage to grieve. We might not often think about how difficult it is in our culture to encourage people to grieve. Many of us become experts in hiding our sorrows and then trying to block out our grief. But it is very important to give ourselves permission to grieve our losses in life so that we

COURAGE AND OUR PERSONALITIES

can have the freedom to truly live. This ability to grieve is another hidden face of courage.

Part of our struggle with grieving is that it goes against many of the stereotypes our culture wants us to live up to. So, in this sense, giving ourselves the freedom to grieve becomes counter cultural. Over the years, I have found that men and women struggle when their opinions, feelings and beliefs conflict with our culture's gender expectations. For example, research on the attributes that we associate with being feminine tells us that some of the most important qualities for women are thin, nice, and modest. That means if women want to play it totally safe, they have to be willing to stay as small, quiet, and attractive as possible. Similarly, when looking at the attributes associated with masculinity, the researchers identified these as important attributes for men: emotional control, primacy of work, and pursuit of status. That means that if men want to play it safe, they need to stop feeling, start earning, and give up on meaningful connections.[20]

In Mitch Albom's book, *Tuesdays with Morrie*, Morrie addressed these kinds of stereotypes that our culture tries to impose on us. Morrie believed that our culture often led people down the wrong path, trying to make people think in certain unhealthy ways. And when that happens, he said that it's important to build your own sub-culture that goes against these stereotypes and gives you life. He expressed his concerns in this way: "the culture we have does not make people feel good about themselves. We're teaching the wrong things. And you have to be strong enough to say if the culture doesn't work, don't buy it. Create your own. Most people can't do it."[21] He went on to explain what he meant by building your own sub-culture. "I don't mean you disregard every rule of your community. I don't go around naked, for example. I don't run through red lights. The little things, I can obey. But the big things—how we think, what we value—those you must choose yourself. You can't let anyone—or any society—determine those for you. And with regard to the stereotypes of men and women in our culture, he said, "it's the same for women not being thin enough, or men not allowing themselves to cry or not ever being rich enough. It's just what our culture would have you believe. Don't believe it."[22]

---

20. Mahalik, "Development of the Conformity to Feminine Norms Inventory," 417–35.

21. Albom, *Tuesdays with Morrie*, 35–36.

22. Ibid., 155.

Sometimes, we surrender who we are because of our cultural ideas of what being a good person is all about. Our true self gets whittled down and measured against some acquired standard of social acceptability. When we are told that "big boys don't cry" and "ladies never disagree with anyone," we learn to disown our feelings and our perspectives. Many of us still hide the parts of ourselves that were unacceptable to our parents or teachers, although our parents are long gone and their work with them. In the world of my childhood, boys never cried. Those that did were sissies. Of course, all girls were supposed to be sissies. However, the world we live in now offers us far greater opportunities for expression, but we may still live in it as if it were the hostile terrain of our childhood.

Life is as complex as we are. Sometimes, our vulnerability is our strength, our fear develops our courage, and our woundedness is the road to our healing. It took Mary a long time to allow herself to grieve. Eventually, it led to her healing.

Mary was an older woman whose husband had died unexpectedly two years before she came to see me. Withdrawn and distant, she had not cried or spoken of his death to anyone in all that time. She no longer cooked or looked after her house or her garden. Most of the time she sat in her bathrobe in the living room, looking out the window. She had been given antidepressants by her doctor but they had not made much difference, and after a while she had simply stopped taking them. "They won't bring him back," she had said. She had been brought to see me by one of her daughters who told me, "I lost both my parents the day my father died."

At first Mary and I sat and looked at each other in silence. She was a lovely woman in her early seventies, but she seemed as lifeless as the chair she sat on. She seemed so fragile that I wondered if she would have the strength to stay the full hour.

I opened the conversation by asking her why she had come. "My husband has died," she replied, turning her head away from me to look out my window. "My daughters would like me to talk about it, but I do not think that I care to." When I gently asked her to say more about this, she said simply, "talking seems a waste of time. No one could possibly understand." I nodded in agreement. "Yes, of course," I said. "You have lost your life. Only your husband could understand what you have lost. Only he knew what your life together was like." At this, she turned back to look at me. Her eyes were grey, like her hair. There was no light in them. I nodded again. "If he were here, Mary, what would you tell him?" I asked her.

Courage and our Personalities

She looked at me for a long moment, Then, she closed her eyes and began to speak to her husband out loud telling him what life was like without him. She told him about going to their special places alone, walking their dogs alone, sleeping in their bed alone. She told him about needing to learn to do the little things he had always taken care of, things she had never known about. She reminded him of times that only he would remember, old memories that no one else had shared. And then for the first time since he died, she began to cry. She cried for a long time.

When the tears stopped, I asked her if there was anything else she had not said. Hesitantly, she told me how angry she was with him for abandoning her to grow old alone. She felt as if he had broken a promise to her. She missed him terribly and all that he had brought into her life.

"He was a teacher of love for me," she told me. The child of rigid and suspicious parents, she had been amazed at her husband's selflessness, his readiness to extend his hand to others, even to strangers. She told me story after story of his generosity, his kindness, her eyes looking beyond me to the past. "Joe always went the extra mile," she said. "So many people loved him."

I was deeply touched by Joe and this woman he had loved. "Mary," I asked her, "if Joe were here, what would he say to you about the way you have lived the last two years of your life?" She looked startled. "Why, he would say 'Mary, why have you built a monument of pain in memory of me? My whole life was about love.'" She paused. Then for the first time, I saw the hint of a smile. "Perhaps there are other ways to remember him," she said.

Afterward, she told me that she had felt that if she let go of her pain, she would betray Joe's memory and diminish the value of his life. She now saw that she had indeed betrayed him by holding on to her pain and closing her heart. She never came back to see me again.

Every great loss demands that we choose life again. And we need the courage to grieve in order to do this. It took a lot of courage for Mary to let go of the way she was grieving that kept her stuck in her pain for over two years. The pain we have not grieved over will always stand between us and life. When we don't grieve, a part of us becomes caught in the past like Lot's wife who, because she looked back, was turned into a pillar of salt.

Grieving is not about forgetting. Grieving allows us to heal, to remember with love rather than pain. It is like a sorting process. One by one you let go of the things that are gone and you mourn for them. One by one you take hold of the things that have become a part of who you are and build again.

About a year after our last meeting, Mary sent me a clipping from the local newspaper about a group of widows she had organized to help elderly people with the tasks they could not do for themselves in their homes. There was no note with the clipping, just a tiny one breath poem she had written and signed: "Grief./I pull up anchor,/and catch the wind." Life is full of painful losses of one kind or another for all of us. It might be the loss of a loved one, a job, a friend or relationship, a position of status in the community, a financial loss. No matter what the loss is, it's important to remember that we cannot protect ourselves from loss. Yet, many people try to employ strategies that they think will protect them from feeling the loss. Over the years in my counseling work, I have especially seen men who struggle with this. But if we try to protect ourselves from grieving the loss, we cannot use the experience to grow, because none of them lead to healing. Although denial, rationalization, substitution, and avoidance may numb the pain of our losses, every one of them hurts us in some far more fundamental ways. None is respectful toward life or toward process. None acknowledges our capacity for finding meaning or wisdom. Pain often marks the place where self-knowledge and growth can happen, much in the same way that fear does.

Grieving is the way our losses can heal. Yet many people do not know how to grieve and heal from their losses. This makes it difficult to find the courage to participate fully in life. At some deep level, it may make us unwilling to be open to others or afraid of becoming attached or intimate with another human being. It may keep us from reaching out and making friends in the future. Many people have become "emotional couch potatoes" because they do not know how to heal their hearts.

It takes a lot of courage to face our losses, our pain, and learn to grieve. But unless we do this, we may need to live life at a distance in order to protect ourselves from pain. We may not be able to risk having anything that really matters to us or allow ourselves to be touched, to be intimate, to care or be cared about. Untouched, we will suffer anyway. We just will not be transformed by our suffering. Grieving may be one of the most fundamental life skills. It is the way the heart can heal from loss and go on to love again and grow wise. If it were up to me, it would be taught in kindergarten, right up there with taking turns and sharing.

COURAGE AND OUR PERSONALITIES

H. The Courage to Become Angry

Freeing a hostage always takes a great deal of courage. But what can keep each of us hostage can be very different. For some people, being taken hostage physically can do tremendous damage to a person. Fortunately, most of us don't have to endure this. However, many other things in life can keep us hostage and make growing in life emotionally and psychologically extremely difficult. For example, addictions keep people hostage and take a tremendous amount of courage to fight and overcome. And our emotions can do the same thing to us. They can keep us hostage until we find a way to break free.

One of the emotions that keep many people hostage is anger. And one of the most interesting and challenging people I have worked with over the years was Joe. Angry and depressed, Joe was actually afraid to get mad. Ever since he was a youngster, anger had been very difficult for him and had caused him a lot of problems. It might seem simplistic, but it took a good deal of courage for him to really express his anger.

This type of struggle with anger has always been very interesting to me in my work as a psychotherapist. For years, in my counseling practice, I have worked with many people who have struggled with this emotion. But, interestingly enough, my work with these clients has usually been devoted to trying to help them understand why anger had been so difficult for them and then helping them learn strategies about how to express angry feelings appropriately. For many of my clients, this emotion has caused significant problems in their lives. But Joe was different. His problem was his fear of anger.

Anger is a difficult emotion to understand. On the one hand, it can be something positive. For example, if we see an injustice being perpetrated, we can have a positive response of anger in order to address the injustice and work for change. On the other hand, it can be a negative dimension in our lives if we don't learn how to control our anger and express it in an appropriate way. Over the years, in my work with others, this has generally been the focus of my efforts.

Anger can cause people many problems. It's not that getting angry is a problem. Anger is just one of our many emotions. It's the expression of our anger that can cause major problems in our lives. For example, in relationships, both at home or at work, angry feelings can be difficult to deal with. If people shout or scream at each other, throw things, etc. anger can be the cause of divorces or cost someone their job. At its worst, an angry person can be dangerous and cause bodily harm to others, even death.

However, for Joe, this emotion had been the opposite of the above. His struggle had been the fear of anger. He was afraid of it and had tried to understand "why" over the years. Now, with the help of our counseling sessions, I think he understands some of the reasons. Joe grew up in a home where his father could become angry very quickly and as he told me, "fly off the handle." Sometimes, he would yell at Joe and his brother. At other times, they "got the belt." This set the stage for his being afraid of anger. His father was also an alcoholic. Joe was also afraid of him then, too, because he never knew how his father was going to act when he was drinking. Another important part of this was the reaction of his mother. Whenever his father was angry and/or drinking, she would become very quiet and withdraw into herself. Emotionally, she would "shut down." This was her way of dealing with his father's anger. And for whatever reason, Joe became like his mother and seemed to develop the same responses she manifested. It's like he dealt with anger the way she did. "I would shut down and become very quiet," he said. He did this as a way of coping with these situations in his home. It was a learned response and the reason he grew up being afraid of anger. He too was afraid of "exploding" and never really learned how to express his anger in an appropriate way.

Coupled with these reasons was the fact that Joe grew up in a religious environment where he was encouraged to not become angry, and certainly never to show it. In his church, anger was seen as a negative emotion, one that was basically bad and needed to be feared—and controlled. Otherwise, this emotion could get you into a lot of trouble. Becoming angry was not acting like Jesus. Of course, Joe knew that Jesus became angry when he drove the money changers out of the Temple but then that didn't really apply to him he thought. He had to learn how to control his anger.

Over the years, anger had been a very difficult emotion for him to deal with and had caused him numerous problems. For example, because anger is such a normal feeling, Joe often became angry at times over many things, but he learned to just "stuff" these feelings—to bury them, to always keep them inside. Because of this, he would often become depressed. Then, like his mother, he would withdraw from the person or situation that caused him to become angry which impacted his relationships in a negative way. This way of handling his angry feelings had been a constant struggle for him. It is why he was afraid of his anger. It is why it took a lot of courage

Courage and our Personalities

for him to express it. It's probably difficult for many people to understand if you haven't grown up in an environment where anger is a major problem. For Joe, it felt like he was never taught how to deal with his angry feelings.

Another issue that flowed from his difficulty with anger was dealing with conflict. Basically, Joe just avoided conflict as much as he could. Similarly, disagreeing with someone on an issue was also very difficult for him. What he had discovered here was that he was afraid that if he got into a conflict with someone or disagreed with someone, it would lead him to become angry and so he avoided it at all costs. But he also came to discover another dimension of his personality in all of this. He came to believe that if he got angry or disagreed with someone, then they wouldn't like him and that could be very threatening for him. It felt like a lot of his self-esteem was tied into this emotion.

Joe was trying to find the courage to live in new ways. As a psychotherapist, I have had the privilege of accompanying many people like Joe, as they have eventually discovered in themselves an unexpected strength, courage beyond what they would have thought possible, an unsuspected sense of compassion, or a capacity for love deeper than they had ever dreamed.

Joe's family had actually cultivated fear. Because of this, emotional survival was a high priority for him. In this environment, Joe had developed strategies to help him cope with the situation. Keeping his anger to himself and avoiding conflict at all costs, helped him survive his family life but never allowed him to grow up emotionally as a person. Joe had been caught in a vicious cycle. Not expressing his anger led to depression and to avoiding conflict which affected his self-esteem in a negative way.

Over our months of working together, Joe realized that in order to break this cycle, he had to learn how to "face into his fear" about anger, which required a great deal of courage on his part. In the beginning, I gave him simple exercises to do where he would practice speaking with me about something that made him angry in a safe environment. Working together, we developed scenarios where he would likely become angry and then practiced responding to these in appropriate ways. Then, we worked on his issue of avoiding conflict. At first, he understood that it was ok to disagree with someone, and that he had a right to his own opinion about things without being punished for it. Gradually, he became more comfortable with this new way of living. His depression lifted and his self-esteem improved.

Many of us have become frozen, trapped by our past. This was certainly true for Joe. It took a lot of time, effort, courage, and emotional energy for him to become more free of his past where he was no longer a hostage. For anyone, freeing a hostage always takes a great deal of courage.

I. The Courage to Follow Our Dreams

In the musical, Les Miserables, Fantine, a poor young woman who is forced by circumstances to become a prostitute, sings a beautiful song entitled, "I Dreamed a Dream." It speaks about her life.

> There was a time when love was blind
> And the world was a song
> And the song was exciting
> There was a time
> Then it all went wrong
> I dreamed a dream in time gone by
> When hope was high
> And life worth living
> I dreamed that love would never die
> I dreamed that God would be forgiving
> Then I was young and unafraid
> And dreams were made and used and wasted. . .
> But there are dreams that cannot be
> And there are storms we cannot weather
> I had a dream my life would be
> So different from this hell I'm living
> So different now from what it seemed
> Now life has killed the dream I dreamed.[23]

Often, it takes a great deal of courage to keep our dreams alive. Why? Because it's not a gentle world. For many people, life is a struggle in so many ways. And these struggles can cause our dreams to die. Everyone goes through difficulties in life of one kind or another. Everyone has sorrows that they struggle with personally or professionally. And, like Fantine,

---

23. This musical is based on the French historical novel by Victor Hugo, first published in 1862. It is generally considered one of the greatest novels of the nineteenth century.

Courage and our Personalities

everyone struggles at times not to let our dreams die—dreams about ourselves, dreams about some part of our life, dreams about some dimension of our world. We don't want to let life kill the dreams we have dreamed.

When I talk about these kinds of dreams, I don't mean some flighty ideas or some passing thought about ourselves or some dimension of our life. It's not saying something to yourself like, "wouldn't it be nice if . . . I were more kind or more loving." Or, "wouldn't it be nice if . . . I could be happier in my job." No, this is not what I mean by holding on to your dreams. It is much more positive than that. What I am talking about here are the dreams, the ideas we have about improving some dimension of our life and then developing a plan to make that dream a reality. When I was in college, I had a dream about getting a Ph.D. but I didn't know if I had the courage, stamina and perseverance to make this a reality. It was probably going to take four more years and I knew it was going to be a difficult journey. As the deadline to apply approached, I decided to talk with one of my professors about the pros and cons of this decision. After he confirmed his belief in me that I could accomplish this goal, he also tried to make me very realistic about how difficult this journey could be and how much courage it would require to face the difficulties that might arise. He gave me some scary statistics about how many people actually finish a doctoral program after beginning it. Then, he scared me even more when he told me how many students actually finish their course work but then never complete their doctoral dissertation. He certainly made me realistic! After that conversation, I had a much better understanding of what it was going to take in order for me to make my dream a reality. After seeking advice from several other people along with more thought and prayer about this decision, I decided to pursue my dream and apply. Fortunately, I was accepted into the program and finished my doctoral degree four years later.

As I reflect back on this period of my life, several things are clear to me. 1) I had a dream, a goal, a desire to obtain a Ph.D. in my profession; 2) I sought the counsel of others to help me sort out the issues so that I could make an informed decision; 3) I tried to be realistic about achieving my goal and developed a plan while taking into consideration how my plan would affect my relationships and my job at the time; 4) I thought and prayed some more and tried to understand how I could find the courage and develop the strategies to handle any problems that might arise. I didn't want any difficulties to kill my dream that I had about this dimension of my life; 5) I was able to struggle with the difficulties as they arose, and was able to persevere in my efforts to achieve my dream.

Emphasizing how difficult it can be to keep our dreams alive, Morrie asked Mitch one time in *Tuesdays with Morrie*, what he wanted to do with his life when he finished college.

"I want to be a musician," Mitch said. "A piano player."

"Wonderful," Morrie replied. "But that's a hard life."

"Yeah."

"A lot of sharks. That's what I hear," Morrie said. "Still, if you really want it, then you'll make your dream happen."[24]

Walt Disney said if you can dream it, you can do it.[25] But sometimes, you need to have the courage to accomplish certain things before you can try and make your dream a reality. This was very true for Judy. She was fifteen when I first began to see her. Her parents brought her to counseling because she was having some emotional and behavioral problems. In one of our first sessions, I asked her what she would like to do with her life. She said she wanted to be a police officer. As we worked together over the ensuing months, Judy was able to understand and deal with her emotional and behavioral issues in a more positive way. We concluded our sessions when she was a senior in high school. After this, I would receive an occasional phone call from her, updating me on how she was doing. Then, about two years ago, she called and wanted to let me know that she had achieved her dream of becoming a police officer. In our sessions together, Judy had exhibited a lot of courage to face her emotional and behavioral issues. After she overcame these in a constructive way, it freed her to pursue her dream.

Judy was just one example of how if you really want something, you work hard to overcome any obstacles to make your dream happen. It took a lot of courage for her to keep her dream alive at times. But she stuck to it and accomplished her goal.

A good example of this process to reflect on might be an oyster. An oyster is soft, tender, and vulnerable. Without the sanctuary of its shell, it could not survive. But oysters must open their shells in order to "breathe" water. They must become vulnerable. Sometimes, while an oyster is breathing, a grain of sand will enter its shell and become a part of its life.

These grains of sand cause pain, but an oyster does not alter its soft nature because of this. It does not become hard and leathery in order not

---

24. Albom, *Tuesdays with Morrie*, 47.
25. https://www.brainyquote.com/quotes/walt_disney_130027.

to feel. It continues on its journey to entrust itself to the ocean, to open and breathe in order to live. However, it finds a way to respond. Slowly and patiently, the oyster wraps the grain of sand in thin translucent layers until, over time, it has created something of great value in its place where it was once most vulnerable to its pain. A pearl might be thought of as an oyster's response to its pain. Of course, not every oyster can do this. Oysters that do are far more valuable to people than oysters that do not.

Sand is a way of life for an oyster. If you are soft and tender and must live on the sandy floor of the ocean, making pearls becomes a necessity if you are to live well. This process of an oyster turning a grain of sand into a pearl is like the process inside of us of turning pain into growth. And the growth that we seek is the ability to hold on to our dreams and not let them die. Our pearl is the wisdom that allows us to persevere through our challenges and disappointments to make our dreams a reality.

J. The Courage to Live with Mystery

Perhaps one of the most difficult things in life to deal with is the unknown. We want answers to our questions about life. We want to know why something happens. We want to know the reason for things that happen to us. My wife and I desperately wanted to know why our son was stillborn. But there are no easy answers to these kinds of questions. They are part of the mystery of life.

The unknown in our lives is always difficult to handle constructively. Most of us are comfortable with what we know. It might be difficult to deal with the known in our lives but at least it doesn't generate the same kind of anxiety that dealing with the unknown does. As the eminent family therapist Virginia Satir said, "most people prefer the certainty of misery to the misery of uncertainty."[26]

One of my favorite quotes is from Rainer Maria Rilke's *Letters to a Young Poet*. Writing to his young friend he said,

> I beg you . . . be patient toward all that is unsolved in your heart and try to love the questions themselves like locked rooms and like books that are written in a very foreign tongue. Do not seek the answers, which cannot be given to you because you would not be able to live them. And the point is, to live everything. Live the

---

26. Quoted in The Family Networker, 13, 30.

questions now. Perhaps you will then gradually, without noticing it, live along some distant day into the answer.[27]

Mystery, by its very nature, cannot be solved, can never be known. Many of us have not been raised to cultivate a sense of mystery. In our society, it is particularly difficult to live with our questions. On the contrary, we are trained to answer questions. We pride ourselves in solving the unknown. We like things fixed, figured out, and nailed down. Some people even see our inability to solve the unknown as an insult to our competence, almost a personal failing. Seen in this way, the unknown becomes a call to action. But mystery does not require action; it requires our attention. Mystery requires that we listen and become open. When we meet with the unknown in this way, we can be touched by a wisdom that can transform our lives.

Jesus was a master at using questions about life to invite people to grow. "What are you looking for?" "Who do you say that I am?" "Do you want to get well?" "Why do you not understand what I say?" "Do you love me?" The New Testament is full of them.

There is an art to living your questions. You feel them. You listen to them. You let them spawn new questions. You hold the unknowing inside. You linger with them instead of rushing into half-baked answers. Jesuit priest and writer Anthony de Mello put it very well: "Some people will never learn anything because they grasp too soon. Wisdom, after all, is not a station you arrive at, but a manner of traveling. . . . To know exactly where you are headed may be the best way to go astray. Not all who loiter are lost."[28]

As a matter of fact, those who "loiter" in the question long enough will "live into" the answer. But we have to be patient. And this waiting can be very difficult. Simone Weil said, "Waiting patiently in expectation is the foundation of the spiritual life."[29] Jesus said, "search, and you will find" (Matt 7: 7). Sometimes, I wonder if this means, "search *long enough*, and you will find." It is the patient art of dwelling in the darkness of a question that eventually unravels the answer. Living our way into the answers to our questions is an invitation to trust more deeply in the Lord's providence. It is believing that even though we cannot always discover satisfying answers to our questions, we know that there is a purpose to them.

27. Rilke, *Letters to a Young Poet*, 34–35.
28. DeMello, *Heart of the Enlightened*, 38.
29. Weil, *First and Last Notebooks*, 99.

Everything and everyone possesses a dimension of the unknown. Mystery helps us to see ourselves and others from the largest possible perspective. To be living is to be unfinished. Nothing and no one is complete. The world and everything in it is *alive*. Reflecting on the importance of mystery in our lives, the well-known anthropologist Jane Goodall said, "How sad it would be . . . if we humans were to loose all sense of mystery, all sense of awe. If our left brains were utterly to dominate the right so that logic and reason triumphed over intuition and alienated us absolutely from our innermost being, from our hearts, our souls."[30]

Finally, it is important to remember that a sense of mystery can take us beyond disappointment and judgment to a place of expectancy. It opens in us an attitude of listening and respect. Mystery requires that we relinquish an endless search for answers and "learn to love the questions themselves." It requires courage and a willingness to not understand everything at times. American author Gilda Radner said, "I wanted a perfect ending. Now I've learned, the hard way, that some poems don't rhyme, and some stories don't have a clear beginning, middle and end. Life is about not knowing, having to change, taking the moment and making the best of it, without knowing what's going to happen next."[31]

Perhaps real wisdom lies in not seeking answers at all. After all my years, I have begun to wonder if the secret of living well is not in having all the answers but in pursuing unanswerable questions in the company of good friends.

K. The Courage to Age Gracefully

Some years ago, Kathy, a colleague of mine, told me an interesting story about one of her clients. Joan, was a fifty-five year old woman who had recently completed her fifth surgery for cervical cancer. In her own mind, she had entered a battle with time, worrying that she didn't have long to live. However, she was also a person who was extremely concerned about her appearance and often enlisted the expertise of a plastic surgeon. With his help, she was able to keep up an appearance of looking much younger than she actually was. Unwilling to grow old, she examined her face and body constantly, exercised daily, and was on a continual diet. "No one really needs to grow old," she told Kathy. "Aging is a choice."

30. Goodall, *Reason for Hope*, ch. 12.
31. https://brainyquote.com/authors/gilda_radner.

Several years after this, Kathy said she was stopped in the grocery store by a pretty gray haired woman that she did not recognize. This lady greeted Kathy warmly. "It's Joan," she said, still chuckling. "I'm growing old. Who would think that someone like me could be so grateful to have wrinkles." If, as Joan said, that aging is a choice, what is it that allows some people to grow old gracefully while others struggle and battle the aging process? Why are some elderly people pleasant and at peace while others appear to be angry and resentful? What are the choices we need to make to allow ourselves to grow old gracefully?

I had the opportunity to experience this process because one of the psychiatrist's at my office was on the staff of a local nursing home. He wanted to try and help the residents by not only giving them their medications, but also providing them with an opportunity to share their lives with each other. So, he asked me to conduct some group counseling sessions with them. For me, it was a very interesting and educational experience. I must say that I think I learned a lot about the aging process just by listening to their stories. As you might expect, some of the residents had grown old gracefully while others were very unhappy and continued to struggle with all kinds of issues. Again, why the difference? What was it that allowed some of them to thrive, while others seemed to deteriorate?

In my work as a psychotherapist for many years, my clients have helped me discover that the ability to grow old gracefully actually begins long before we are actually "old." In my work, I have found at least four important elements in growing old gracefully. There are probably more. It is important to understand these in order to help prepare ourselves.

1. *Negotiating the transitions of life in a positive way.* We don't wake up one morning as an elderly person and say to ourselves that "today we are going to begin to age gracefully." No. Rather, it is a phase of life that we grow into by successfully negotiating the various transitions in our earlier years. And doing this requires a lot of courage. It is one of those hidden faces of courage. For example, coming through the transitions of midlife can become very important because this allows us to begin the process of aging gracefully. Commenting on this process of growing older, famous Swiss psychiatrist Carl Jung believed that every midlife crisis is a spiritual crisis, that we are called to die to the old self (ego), the fruit of the first half of life and liberate the new man or woman within us. He said,

> Wholly unprepared, they embark upon the second half of life. Or are there perhaps colleges for forty-year-olds which prepare them

for their coming life and its demands as the ordinary colleges introduce our young people to a knowledge of the world and of life? No, there are none. Thoroughly unprepared we take the step into the afternoon of life; worse still, we take this step with the false presupposition that our truths and ideas will serve as hitherto. But we cannot live the afternoon of life according to the program of life's morning—for what was great in the morning will be little at evening, and what in the morning was true will at evening have become a lie.[32]

Jung divided life into two phases. The first phase, or morning," is reserved for relating and orienting to the outer world by developing the ego. The second half, or "afternoon," is for adapting to the inner world by developing the full and true self. The midlife transition between these two Jung likened to a difficult birth. However, if we can negotiate these midlife transitions well by the choices we make, it will allow us to begin the process of aging gracefully.

The reason these midlife transitions can be difficult and require courage is because it involves a real breakdown of our old spiritual and psychic structures—the old masks and persons that have served us well in the past but no longer fit. The overarching roles that created the theme song for our lives begin to lose their music. It feels like anguish to come to that place in life where you know all the words but none of the music.

In our youth, we set up inner myths and stories to live by, but around the midlife juncture these patterns begin to crumble. It feels to us like a collapsing of all that is, but it's a holy quaking. "When order crumbles," writes John Shea, "mystery rises."[33]

One of my favorite Scripture passages comes from Ecclesiastes: "To everything there is a season, and a time for every purpose under heaven: a time to be born, and a time to die; a time to plant, and a time to pluck up that which is planted" (Eccl 3: 1–2). We need courage and reassurance that it's okay to let the old masks die, to "pluck up" what was planted long ago.

A friend reminded me a long time ago, "if you think God leads you only besides still waters, think again. God will also lead you beside turbulent waters. If you have the courage to enter, you'll think you're drowning. But actually you're being churned into something new. It's okay, dive in."

Jung also believed that we all have a "shadow"; it's the rejected, inferior person inside we have always ignored and fought becoming. But when this

---

32. Jung, "Stages of Life," 783.
33. Shea, *Stories of God*, 29.

fullness of time comes to each of us, a sacred voice at the heart of us cries out, shaking the old foundation. It draws us into a turbulence that forces us to confront our deepest issues. It's as if some inner, divine grace seeks our growth and will plunge us, if need be, into a cauldron that seethes with questions and voices we would just as soon not hear. One way or another, the false roles, identities, and illusions spill over the sides of our life, and we are forced to stand in the chaos.

Without such upheaval, we would likely go on as always. It's so like us to deny things until some jolting moment—something we call an "eye-opening" experience—comes along and sharpens our vision.

"There is a self within each of us aching to be born," says theologian Alan Jones.[34] And when this aching breaks into our lives—whether through a midlife struggle or some other crisis—we must somehow find the courage to say yes.

Traveling through these turbulent transitions takes courage. It's like coming out of a storm into calmer waters. But this can be difficult because we tend to "stay put," rather than push out into the deep—into new territory. However, if we can negotiate these transitions in a positive way, it will be the beginning of moving into the second half of life in a healthy way. Then, as we continue to grow and mature, the stage will be set for us to age gracefully. Personally, we will feel more real, more integrated, more unified. We will feel like our true selves are finally emerging. There will no longer be a need to wear our masks that got us through the first half of life. And because we will feel more personally authentic, we know these changes in ourselves can have tremendous implications for our relationships. Just like with ourselves, we can be more genuine and authentic with our friends. With them too, we will no longer need to wear any masks and we can "let them in," so to speak, to see "the real me." This freedom to be our true self allows our friendships to mature and deepen. This is one of the reasons why, as we grow older and become more mature, some people feel a new birth within themselves that not only enhances their own personal lives but opens up many opportunities for friendships. Reflecting on the later stages of life, the poet Robert Browning wrote, "Come grow old with me, the best is yet to be."[35]

2. *Embrace the aging process.* The second element that is needed to grow old gracefully is to embrace the aging process. And this takes courage.

---

34. Jones, *Journey into Christ*, 52.
35. Quotegems.com/love-proverbs/robertbrowning.

Courage and our Personalities

So many of us fear it. In our culture, there is such an emphasis on youth. Just look at the advertisements that surround us. Young and beautiful people trying to sell us everything from shampoo to clothes, cars, and food.

Speaking about this challenging dimension of life, Morrie told Mitch in *Tuesdays with Morrie*,

> all this emphasis on youth—I don't buy it. Listen, I know what a misery being young can be, so don't tell me it's so great. All these kids who came to me with their struggles, their strife, their feelings of inadequacy, their sense that life was miserable, so bad they wanted to kill themselves.... And, in addition to all the miseries, the young are not wise. They have very little understanding about life. Who wants to live every day when you don't know what's going on? When people are manipulating you, telling you to buy this perfume and you'll be beautiful, or this pair of jeans and you'll be sexy—and you believe them! It's such nonsense.
>
> Weren't you *ever* afraid to grow old? Mitch asked.
>
> Mitch, I *embrace* aging. Embrace it?
>
> It's very simple. As you grow, you learn more. If you stayed at twenty-two, you'd always be as ignorant as you were at twenty-two. Aging is not just decay, you know. It's growth. It's more than the negative that you're going to die, it's also the positive that you *understand* you're going to die, and that you live a better life because of it.
>
> Yes, Mitch said, but if aging were so valuable, why do people always say, oh, if I were young again. You never hear people say, I wish I were sixty-five.
>
> Morrie smiled. You know what that reflects? Unsatisfied lives. Unfulfilled lives. Lives that haven't found meaning. Because if you've found meaning in your life, you don't want to go back. You want to go forward. You want to see more, do more. You can't wait until sixty-five. Listen. You should know something. All younger people should know something. If you're always battling against getting older, you're going to be unhappy, because it will happen anyhow.
>
> So then Mitch asked him if he ever envied younger, healthy people.
>
> Oh, I guess I do. I envy them being able to go to the health club, or go for a swim, or dance. Mostly for dancing. But if envy comes to me, I feel it, and then I let it go. It's impossible for the old not to

envy the young. But the issue is to accept who you are and revel in that. This is your time to be in your thirties. I had my time to be in my thirties, and now is my time to be seventy-eight. You have to find what's good and true and beautiful in your life as it is now. Looking back makes you competitive. And, age is not a competitive issue. The truth is, part of me is every age. I'm a thirty-three year old, I'm a five year old, I'm a thirty-seven year old, I'm a fifty year old. I've been through all of them, and I know what it's like. I delight in being a child when it's appropriate to be a child. I delight in being a wise old man when it's appropriate to be a wise old man. Think of all I can be! I am every age, up to my own.[36]

3. *Find meaning in your life.* I have also learned from my clients that in order to have the courage to grow old gracefully, you have to find meaning in your life. Then, as we move through the years, aging gracefully becomes an ongoing extension and culmination of a life well lived.

There is a story about a little wave bobbing along in the ocean, having a grand old time. He's enjoying the wind and the fresh air—until he notices the other waves in front of him, crashing against the shore.

"My God, this is terrible," the wave says. "Look what's going to happen me!"

Then along comes another wave. It sees the first wave, looking grim, and it says to him, 'why do you look so sad?'

The first wave says, 'you don't understand! We're all going to crash! All of us waves are going to be nothing! Isn't it terrible?'

The second wave says, 'no, you don't understand. You're not a wave, you're part of the ocean.'"

Moving into our twilight years, growing old gracefully, gives us the freedom and wisdom about life that helps us to realize that we are part of the ocean. With the ebb and flow of our years, it allows us to give back to others and do our part to make the world a better place.

People who have found meaning in their lives and have aged gracefully have a kind of wisdom about life that can be very helpful to younger people. In our western culture, we tend to value being young and achieving. But in Japanese and Korean society, elderly people are loved and respected. Some years ago, a friend was asked by his Korean friend when he would be turning seventy. His Korean friend told him, "when you get old and weak, please come to Korea and we will take care of you. When you get older, you are more valuable and wonderful. So, please come and live with us. We will

---

36. Albom, *Tuesdays with Morrie*, 120.

make all the necessary arrangements." They want to tap into the wisdom of the aging.

4. *Forgiveness and aging gracefully.* The fourth and maybe one of the most important elements involved in growing old gracefully is choosing to forgive. I saw this in my work with many of the patients in the nursing home. Those who had struggled to forgive were somehow more peaceful than those that hadn't forgiven. Those who had not forgiven others or themselves, seemed to hold on to hurts and grudges. Sometimes, these hurts seemed to consume them. They took up so much emotional energy that there was no way they could grow old gracefully. They were angry, bitter people. Those who had forgiven seemed to be more at peace and able to enjoy life. This helped them to grow old gracefully.

Stanislaw Lac once said, "youth is a gift of nature, but age is a work of art."[37] And to age gracefully, is to bring our life to fulfillment.

---

37. https://brainyquote.com/quotes/stanislaw_jerzy_lec120623.

3

The Courage to "Let Go"

"There is a crack in everything. That's how the light gets in." Anthem

Theologian Mary Daly wrote, "courage is like—it's a habitus, a habit, a virtue: you get it by courageous acts. It's like you learn to swim by swimming. You learn courage by "couraging."[1] In a similar way, the ancient philosopher Aristotle said that we become brave by doing brave acts. But what are brave acts? Often times, people might think that courage—doing brave acts—takes place outside ourselves. While this is sometimes the case, it has also been my experience in working with many people in counseling, that courage often takes place quietly, inside ourselves, as people work on their issues that have been problematic for them, sometimes for a long time. Other people might never hear or see their courage, but it is truly there, present each day.

In sharing their stories with me, my clients have taught me that one of the most difficult and challenging things to do in life is to "let go." Sometimes, an idea, a belief, an opinion, a way of thinking about some aspect of life can stunt our growth and keep us from growing emotionally, psychologically, and spiritually. This kind of "letting go," is often an "undoing" rather than a "doing," a freeing ourselves from beliefs we have about who we are and ways we have been persuaded to "fix" ourselves. Trying to "let go" of things in our lives that are not allowing us to grow requires a great

1. www.azquotes.com/author/3603-mary_daly.

deal of courage. However, if we can enter into this process of "letting go," my clients have also shown me how much growth is possible when we have the courage to face these dimensions of our lives.

So, what are the aspects of our lives that we need to "let go" of? What are the dimensions of our lives that tend to hold us back from growing? While the following ideas are certainly not an exhaustive list, they are the ones that I have seen repeated over and over again by my clients.

Sam was twenty-one when he died in a car accident. His mother, who was devastated, told me that she kept one of his shirts in the bottom of her clothes hamper as a way of remembering him. Year after year she left it there—for about five years. It was one of her ways of trying to hang on to him. Then, one day her daughter came over and did the laundry, including her brother's shirt. When the mother saw his clean shirt hanging in the closet, she said she felt somewhat surprised but she didn't feel sorrow or disappointment. For her, it seemed to be the right time for the shirt to leave the dirty clothes hamper. As she reflected on this experience, she came to believe that for her it was a symbol of progress—that she was getting better and beginning to "let go."

Many times, there is a tension between "holding on" and "letting go." And this includes not only material things, as we will see, but other dimensions of life as well. It can be a painful struggle and usually takes time. Often, it requires a lot of patience and courage.

Sometimes, we might need to hold on to someone or some dimension of our life for a period of time until the time is right and then we can let go. This is the way it was for Sam's mother. If other people knew that she had left his shirt in the hamper for five years, they might have thought that she was losing it! But she needed that time to work through her grief and then she could let go. And, this is the way it is for all of us. We all have our own time table for working through challenging situations, and what might work well for one person will not be good for another. For Sam's mother, holding on to the dirty shirt served a purpose in her life. And for us, sometimes holding on serves a psychological purpose or has a particular meaning in our lives.

Holding on tends to make us feel safe, secure and in control of our lives while letting go can make us feel like we are drifting, insecure and losing control. For some, it's a personality issue and can lead to serious problems. Hoarders are probably the people at the extreme end of the spectrum. But fortunately most of us are not afflicted with this kind of problem.

Nevertheless, most of us struggle with this dimension of life to some degree. It's probably true to say that the areas of life we tend to cling to are personal to each one of us. However, there are also other areas which are often difficult and challenging to most of us. Let me just mention several of them.

A. The Courage to Let Go of Our False Selves and Embrace Who We Are

I have discovered in my work with others that many of us are afraid to let our true selves be seen and known. This is why Dag Hammarskjold said that "the longest journey is the journey inwards."[2] We all struggle to some degree with shame and the fear of not being enough. It's difficult, certainly challenging, and requires courage to let go of who you think you are supposed to be and to embrace who you are.

How can we wake up in the morning and think that no matter what gets done today and how much is left undone, I am enough? How do we go to bed each night thinking, yes I am imperfect and vulnerable and sometimes afraid, but that doesn't change the truth that I am also brave and courageous and worthy of love and belonging?

My clients have helped me understand that owning our story can be hard work but not nearly as difficult as spending our lives running from it. Embracing our vulnerabilities is risky but not nearly as dangerous as giving up on love and belonging and joy—the experiences that make us the most vulnerable. Only when we have the courage and are brave enough to explore the darkness will we discover the infinite power of our light.

Embracing who we are requires a lot of courage. It is truly one of those hidden faces of courage that all of us have to deal with. The root of the word courage is *cor*—the Latin word for heart. In one of its earliest forms, the word courage had a very different definition than it does today. Courage originally meant, "to speak one's mind by telling all one's heart."[3] Over time, this definition has changed, and today, courage is more synonymous with being heroic. As we have seen, heroics are important and we certainly need heroes, but I think we've lost touch with the idea that speaking honestly and openly about who we are, about what we're feeling, and about our experiences, good and bad, is the definition of courage. Heroics is often

---

2. Hammarskjold, *Markings*, 65.
3. https://www.goodreads.com.brenebrown.

about putting our life on the line. Ordinary courage is about putting our vulnerability on the line. In today's world, that's pretty extraordinary.

My clients have also helped me to understand that love and belonging are essential to the human experience. But in order to experience love and belonging, we have to believe that we are worthy of love and belonging. So many people doubt this about themselves.

When we let go of what other people think and believe in ourselves, we gain access to the feeling that we are good enough just as we are and that we are worthy of love and belonging. However, when we spend a lifetime trying to distance ourselves from the parts of our lives that don't fit with who we think we are supposed to be, we stand outside ourselves and look for our worthiness by constantly doing what I call the four "p's:" 1) performing; 2) perfecting; 3) pleasing; 4) and proving. Our sense of being enough, that critically important piece that gives us access to love and belonging lives inside of us, not outside of ourselves.

The greatest challenge for most of us is believing that we are worthy *now*, right at this moment. But many of us don't believe this about ourselves. Many of us have a list of "worthiness prerequisites."

"I'll be worthy when I lose twenty-five pounds."

"I'll be worthy if everyone thinks I'm a good parent."

"I'll be worthy if I can hold my marriage together."

"I'll be worthy when I get the next promotion."

"I'll be worthy when my parents finally approve."

Our list can be endless. But the point is—is that we are worthy *now*, not after we fix something in ourselves.

In order for us to embrace who we are, we have to understand the difference between "fitting in" and "belonging." Many of us use these terms interchangeably and generally speaking, we are really good at fitting in. We know exactly how to act in order to get approval and acceptance. We know what to wear, what to talk about, how to make people happy, as well as what not to mention.

However, it is important to understand that "fitting in" and "belonging" are not the same thing. In fact, fitting in often gets in the way of belonging. Fitting in is about assessing a situation and becoming who you need to be, to be accepted. It's like being a chameleon as we journey through the day. Belonging, on the other hand, doesn't require us to "change" who we are. It requires us "to be" who we are.

Love always belongs with belonging. In fact, a deep sense of love and belonging is an irreducible need of everyone. We are biologically, cognitively, physically, and spiritually wired to love, to be loved, and to belong. My clients have shown me that when those needs are not met, we don't function very well. We break. We numb. We lash out. We hurt others. We get sick. There are certainly other causes of illness, numbing, and hurt, but the absence of love and belonging will always lead to suffering, problems and difficulties.

It is important to understand that we cultivate love and belonging when we allow our most vulnerable selves to be deeply seen and known. Love is not something we simply give or get. Rather, it is something that we nurture and grow and can only be cultivated between two people when it exists within each one of them. We can only love others as much as we love ourselves. Shame, blame, disrespect, and the withholding of affection, damage the roots from which love grows. Love can only survive these injuries if they are acknowledged and healed.

If you look at these ideas about love and think about what it means in terms of self-love, it's very specific. Practicing self-love means learning how to trust ourselves, to treat ourselves with respect, and to be kind and affectionate toward ourselves. This is very difficult given how hard most of us are on ourselves. So many of us talk to ourselves in ways that we would never talk to someone else. For example, many of us are quick to think, "God, I'm so stupid," and "man, I'm such an idiot." Just like calling someone we love stupid or an idiot would be incongruent with practicing love, talking like that to ourselves takes a serious toll on our self-love.

"Belonging" is what we long for, "fitting in" is often what we try to do. Moreover, belonging is the innate human desire to be part of something larger than ourselves.

Because this yearning is so basic, we often try to acquire it by fitting in and by seeking approval. These are not only hollow substitutes for belonging, but often real barriers to it. Because true belonging only happens when we present our authentic, imperfect selves to the world, our sense of belonging can never be greater than our level of self-acceptance.

After working with clients for many years, I am convinced that the desire to belong is in our DNA. It is most likely connected to our most primitive survival instinct. Sometimes, it's a teenager wanting to feel like they belong in a family, sometimes, it's a person at work, wanting to feel as though they belong to a group of co-workers, sometimes, it's a person wanting to feel as though they belong in a community or to a particular organization. However, given how difficult it is to cultivate self-acceptance in our perfectionistic society and how our need for belonging is hardwired, it is no wonder that we spend our lives trying to fit in and gain approval. It is so much easier to say, "I'll be whoever or whatever you need me to be, as long as I feel like I'm part of this." From gangs to gossiping, we'll do what it takes to fit in, if we believe it will meet our need for belonging. But it doesn't. We can only belong when we offer our most authentic selves and when we are embraced for who we are. This is why loving and accepting ourselves are the ultimate acts of courage.

When we understand these important ideas about love and belonging, they will help us to fundamentally change the way we live. We will then begin to see how important they are to truly practice them. For most of us, if we are tired and stressed, we can be mean and hurtful, especially to the people we are closest to, like our spouse, our kids, the people we work with. But if we say we truly love them, then how we *behave* every day is as important, if not more important, than simply saying, "I love you" every day. When we don't practice love with the people we claim to love, it takes a lot out of us. Incongruent living can be exhausting.

Sometimes, simply being accepted as you are and cared about by others can affect people in very profound ways. In fact, other people can help us understand the importance of belonging and the significance of accepting ourselves just as we are. One time in a retreat that I participated in, a sand-tray box was used and the eight people on the retreat had the opportunity to choose objects from a sand-tray room that somehow represented what was important to them in life and then to use these objects to share this meaning with each other.

Joan, a young lawyer, took part in one of these sessions. As each person seated around the sand-tray table placed the objects they had gathered into their section of the sand, I noticed that she kept something back and put it under her chair. Because the instruction was to use all the symbols you brought to the table, I had wondered why she had done this. One by one, the group members spoke about the objects they had chosen and shared how each object symbolized what was important to them. Joan listened closely and seemed deeply moved by what the others were saying. About halfway through, she began to speak about what she had put in front of her in the sand. When she finished, she fell silent for a few moments and then hesitantly told us there was something she wanted to add that she did not want others to see. She asked us to close our eyes while she did this.

Everyone closed their eyes. In the silence, Joan reached under her chair for the object she had hidden. After a few moments, she told us we could open our eyes, and we saw that she had placed a slender white candle in a tall candlestick in the center of her part of the sand-tray. It was unlit. Just showing it to us obviously had a deep emotional significance for her. Another retreatant offered her a box of matches, and she sat holding them for a long time, unable to light the candle or even talk about it. Finally, she lit it, saying in a barely audible voice that it represented her real, authentic self. It was a touching moment, especially powerful because the candle bore a striking resemblance to her own beauty and simplicity.

One at a time, others also shared the meaning of their objects, and then the woman seated next to Joan at the table began to speak. She, too, had an unlit candle in her tray. It was short and fat. She told us that it represented her dream of being a professional and truly wanting to help others. As she spoke, instead of lighting her candle with the matches, she picked it up, reached across the low wooden boundary between her section of the table and Joan's and lit it from the flame of Joan's candle. Joan burst into tears.

Then, this woman began to apologize, saying that she had no idea why she had not used the matches and had not meant to invade Joan's sand-tray. "Oh no," Joan told her, "it's that there is usually so much cynicism and judgment among us that I never show anyone at work what really matters to me. Only my very good friends know. I am afraid that people will laugh or that they will think less of me and so I hide myself. For me, my work is holy. It is my calling. When you lit your candle from mine, I saw why it might be important to stop hiding. Perhaps I can find the courage to be who I really am. Perhaps there are others who are hiding too." There was a moment of silence, and then these two women reached for each other's hands.

Embracing our lives, accepting ourselves and becoming who we truly are meant to be requires much courage and many choices. Sometimes, these choices help us to stop hiding and enable us to become the person we want to be. Christopher Germer said that "a moment of self-compassion can change your entire day. A string of such moments can change the course of your life."[4] This is why self-compassion can be extremely helpful in letting go of who we think we are supposed to be and embrace who

---

4. https://goodreads.com/quotes/christophergermer.

we are. It allows us to integrate those parts of ourselves that we struggle with in a positive way so that we can grow into the person we want to be. And, in order to develop this kind of self-compassion, we need two things: 1) self-kindness, and 2) emotional balance. Self-kindness means being warm and understanding toward ourselves when we fail or feel inadequate, rather than ignoring our faults or beating ourselves up with self-criticism. Emotional balance recognizes that suffering and feelings of personal inadequacies are part of our shared human experience. It's something we all go through rather than something that happens to "me" alone. It also means taking a balanced approach to negative emotions so that these kinds of feelings are neither suppressed nor exaggerated. Finally, emotional balance requires that we not "over-identify" with thoughts and feelings, so that we are caught up and swept away by negativity. I think these ideas are key for those of us who struggle with being perfect and getting down on ourselves.

Most of us are trying to live authentic lives and become the person God wants us to be. Deep down, we want to stop pretending and be real and imperfect. There is a line from Leonard Cohen's song "Anthem" that serves as a reminder to me when I get into that place where I'm trying to control everything and make it perfect. The line is, "there is a crack in everything. That's how the light gets in."[5] So many of us run around trying to spackle all the cracks, trying to make everything look just right. This line can help us remember the beauty of the cracks—like the messy house, the imperfect manuscript, and the jeans that are too tight. It reminds us that our imperfections and shortcomings are not inadequacies. They are simply reminders that we are all in this together. Imperfectly, but together.

B. The Courage to Let Go of our Need for Approval

One personality or psychological issue that can become problematic for us and require a lot of courage to face is our excessive need for approval. Because we are social beings, it is quite normal for us to seek the approval of our parents, a spouse, a friend, or the boss at work. Basically, there is nothing wrong with this and it can be growthful if it's done in a healthy way. However, if this is done too much, it can become very debilitating. If we cling to this need for the approval of others, it can be stifling psychologically and can limit our ability to function freely as a person. If we live our lives needing this person or that person to approve of us, it can cramp

---

5. https://genius.com/leonardcohen.

our freedom to live our lives as unique individuals. If we go through life wondering if someone agrees with us or not, it limits our ability to make our own decisions. And, if we need the approval of others too much, it can put a lot of stress on us and make you feel like you are in a box, trapped.

Perhaps another way of thinking about this is to ask yourself the question: "what will others think of me, if I . . . ? If we cannot act without them thinking well of us, then we are limiting our freedom and our ability to make free choices. However, it is also important to remember that we don't live in a vacuum and how others think of us and our need for other's approval can be a good thing. It only becomes a problem when it becomes too excessive in our personalities. And so, letting go of the need for the approval of others and not clinging or worrying about what others think about us can bring a lot of interior freedom.

Maybe what we need to do is to learn how to set new boundaries and begin to let go of our need to please, perform, and be perfect. For example, maybe we need to start by saying "no" sometimes to someone or something we don't really want to do rather than saying "yes" and then being angry and resentful later on.

Letting go of this excessive need for approval, can be a sign of growth and maturity. If we hold on too tightly or for too long to people or situations, it can be detrimental to us. This is often true in relationships and career issues. In our relationships, sometimes it's difficult to let go. This seems to be especially true in friendships. We can tend to hold on to friendships for all kinds of reasons, even when we begin to suspect that we should let go of the person. But this usually takes time and we need to be patient with ourselves as we move through the issues involved in order to make a good decision. This can certainly be a painful process because most of us don't develop good friendships quickly or drop them easily. However, it also takes a lot of strength and courage to leave a friendship or put new boundaries on one when we realize that this would be for the best. This is when letting go can be very important. When a relationship or friendship is no longer healthy for whatever reason, or is not life-giving to you or the other person, it is time to let go and move on. American political writer, Theodore H. White realized how difficult this could be when he wrote, "to go against the dominant thinking of your friends, of most of the people you see every day, is perhaps the most difficult act of heroism you can have."[6]

---

6. https://goodreads.com/quotes/theodorehwhite.

Or, how about career issues? If you are no longer happy in your career or job, do we simply hold on to it or let go and move on to something else? These can be very difficult decisions that can take time to resolve. Again, we need to be patient with ourselves as we sort through the issues involved and come to the best decision for ourselves. And with this type of situation, there are obviously many practical dimensions that we will need to consider.

C. The Courage to Let Go of Comparison

Many years ago, I participated in a retreat where one of the first topics we talked about was what it was like growing up in our families of origin and the impact this had on our lives. I can still remember how Paula's story impacted her life and made me think about my own.

Paula said that some of her best childhood memories were from her early years when her family lived outside of Chicago, in a small duplex house, a couple of blocks from Loyola University. She said she remembered her mom and herself spending hours making crafts with her friends.

As she shared her story, she said she could vividly see her mother and her friends coming home from the grocery store and making all kinds of delicious food. She said she was so fascinated with helping her mother in the kitchen that one Sunday afternoon her mom let her cook alone. Her mother told her she could make anything she wanted with any ingredients that she wanted to use. She said she made oatmeal raisin cookies with crawfish boil spices instead of cinnamon. The entire house stank for days!

Paula went on to say that her mother loved to sew. She made matching dresses that she and her mother wore, along with her doll, who also had her own tiny matching dress. These also held some wonderful memories for her.

Sadly, things changed for her family around the age of eight or nine. That was about the time that they moved from their tiny house near Chicago to a big house in a sprawling Dallas suburb. Everything in her family seemed to change then. In Chicago, every wall in her house was covered with art done by her mother, herself, or one of her siblings. Homemade curtains hung over every window. Although they were very plain, she remembered them as being beautiful.

In Dallas, Paula remembered walking into some of her neighbors' houses and thinking that their living rooms looked like the lobby of a fancy hotel. There were long heavy drapes, big sofas with matching chairs, and shiny glass tables. There were plastic plants with hanging vines and dried flowers in baskets decorating the tops of tables. Strangely, she thought, everyone's lobby kind of looked the same.

She went on to say that while the houses seemed to be the same and pretty fancy, her school was a different story. In Chicago, she said she went to a Catholic school and everyone looked the same, prayed the same, and, for the most part, acted the same. However, in Dallas, she went to a public school, which meant no more uniforms. In this new school, cute clothes were important. And not homemade cute clothes, but clothes from "the mall."

In Chicago, she said her dad worked during the day and was a law student at Loyola University at night. There was always an informal and fun feeling to their lives. Once they got to Dallas, he dressed up every morning and commuted to the oil and gas company along with almost every other father in the neighborhood. Things changed, Paula said, and in many ways that move felt like a fundamental shift for her family. Her parents were launched on the "accomplishments-and-acquisitions" track, and creativity gave way to that stifling combination of "fitting in" and "being better than," also known as comparison.

Comparison is all about conformity and competition. At first, it seems like conforming and competing are mutually exclusive, but they're not. When we compare, we want to see who or what is best out of a specific collection of things that are alike. We may compare things like how we parent with parents who have totally different values or traditions than us. However, the comparisons that usually get us really riled up are the ones we make with the folks living next door, or on our child's soccer team, or at our school. Most of us don't compare our houses to the mansions across town. We compare our yard to the yards on our block. When we compare, we want to be the best or have the best of our group.

The comparison mandate becomes this crushing paradox of "fit in and stand out!" It's not cultivate self-acceptance, belonging, and authenticity. It's just be like everyone else, but better. That's why it takes courage to "let go" of our need to compare. To be satisfied with who we are, what we have, and happy to be our unique individual selves.

Laura Williams says, "comparison is the thief of happiness."[7] So often, people have told me that they are feeling good about themselves and their

---

7. https://www.thriveglobal.com/stories/how-to-be-happy.

families, and then, in a split second it's gone, because consciously or unconsciously they start comparing themselves to other people. It's easy to see how difficult it is to make time for the important things such as creativity, gratitude, joy, and authenticity when you're spending enormous amounts of time and energy conforming and competing.

Charlie told me that he had spent most of his life comparing himself to others. Did he make more money than his friends? Was he more popular than others? Then, as he rose through the ranks of his company to become an executive, he wondered if he was more intelligent than his peers? Sexier? Did others sit on more powerful boards of directors than he did? In short, comparing himself to others had been a way of life for Charlie.

All this changed when he got sick with prostate cancer. And, in the midst of his radiation treatments, he also became very depressed. That is when I began to see Charlie for counseling. During the following months, he came to understand himself better. As he reflected on his life, he said that comparing himself to others had always been a way of life for him. This is where he got his self-esteem—by seeing himself as "better than" others. He was never quite "good enough" himself. Moreover, he said that his father had always been this way and he could remember numerous times in his early years when his father was always comparing himself to his neighbors in one way or another. Then, in high school, Charlie, who was a good athlete, compared himself to the other players on his football team and to several of his friends, as to who had the prettiest and most popular girl friend. These were the ways that he felt good about himself. However, he was not sure anymore that this was the way he wanted to continue living his life.

During the course of our discussions, I suggested that Charlie begin to do a morning reflection each day. He had never done this before. As he did this each day, he came to understand that the most important quality of his life was his own uniqueness. "Each of us is one of a kind," he said. None of us has existed in the history of the human race before. This realization on his part gave him a profound sense of peace and an unfamiliar acceptance of himself as he was. His self-esteem was based on the kind of person he was and not on any external comparisons with others.

Gradually, Charlie also said that he began to look at others differently. He was trying to listen to others with a new respect, wanting to know the ways in which they were unique. What he used to perceive as differences to be judged and possibly dismissed, he now saw as their uniqueness to be appreciated and understood. He learned a great deal of value from people whom he would barely have noticed before. Now, he made fewer comparisons.

One of the reasons it takes a lot of courage not to get into the "comparison rat race" is because it is so much a part of our culture. We grow up comparing ourselves to others in all kinds of ways. Who is more popular? Who has the best grades? Who has the prettiest girl friend? Who's is the best athlete? Who has the best job? Makes the most money? Has the biggest house? Who has the most friends? It goes on and on. This is why it takes a lot of courage to get off this train and be your own person.

Over the years, I have witnessed in the lives of the people I have worked with in counseling, how detrimental comparisons can be. They hardly ever have any lasting positive effects. Rather, comparisons often lead to envy, jealously, gossiping, anger, tearing others down, resentments, and depression. These never have good outcomes. While some people might get a temporary high from feeling they are "better than" others, these feelings often dissipate as we live our daily lives.

In order to leave the competition and comparison game, we need to do three things. First, recognize and appreciate our own goodness and uniqueness. This is what Charlie began to do. Realizing that there is only one of "me" and one of "you," can give us a new appreciation of ourselves and others, so that our self-esteem comes from within ourselves, rather than outside ourselves. In his book, *Living An Examined Life,* James Hollis said, "each of us has a gift, the essential gift of being who we are, with all the flaws, shortcomings, mistakes and fears of which we are all so aware.... We are all here to be ourselves.... And our gift to the great mosaic of the world is our uniqueness. Each of us has something to bring to the mosaic of time that is unfolding in and through us whether we are aware of it or not."[8] Often, there is great relief in knowing that we don't need to compare and compete.

A second thing that can help us get off the comparison bandwagon is appreciating others and rejoicing with them in their own goodness and successes. In fact, we strengthen the life in others any time we listen generously or encourage others to find meaning in their lives or help them escape from self-judgment and inner criticism. Any time we share someone's joy and help them know that they are important, we bless the life in them.

---

8. Hollis, *Living an Examined Life,* 51.

The Courage to "Let Go"

Jennifer does this as naturally as she breathes. Although her own life has not been easy, she is nonetheless a celebrator, a deeply happy person. Although she has had two episodes of colon cancer and many professional disappointments, her joy in life is tangible. I smile whenever I am in the same room with her. She is always one of the first to celebrate someone's birthday, to remember anniversaries, to congratulate people on their successes, whether she knows them well or not. So Jennifer is one of the first people to call when something good happens to you or to someone you love. She is there to listen to the whole story with delight. Often, when you finish talking to her, you feel even better about what has happened, luckier than before.

Once I asked her about her joy in life. Her own life had been so hard. Didn't she feel envious of others who had things she didn't? She smiled at the thought and shook her head. "Then what is your secret?" I asked. She replied that it seemed to her that joy was not something personal. When I looked at her, puzzled, she explained she has found that if you are genuinely happy for others, people are very generous with their joy and share it with you openheartedly. "When something good happens to the person next to me, I am there to celebrate it with them. Their good luck makes me feel lucky. I rejoice with them about it as fully as if it was happening to me," she told me. "It makes me really happy." She paused and looked thoughtful. "Of course, then it *is* happening to me," she said with a grin. Rejoicing with others in who they are as well as their successes allows us to get off the comparison bandwagon. What a relief this can be.

A third thing that we can do to leave the competition and comparison game is to cultivate a grateful heart. Develop an "attitude of gratitude." If we can focus on our many blessings in life each day, this will allow us to become more grateful. The well known English writer G. K. Chesterton once wrote: "nothing taken for granted; everything received with gratitude; everything passed on with grace."[9] So, the question becomes, how can we learn to receive everything with gratitude and pass it on with grace?

While there might be a variety of ways of accomplishing this, I have found that growing in a life of gratitude and cultivating a grateful heart requires us to deepen our awareness of life. For most of us, this is not easy. It requires work. But the effort we put into this endeavor can bear tremendous fruit. There are numerous, practical ways of doing this. One of the ways I have found helpful over the years is to suggest to people that they review

---

9. Kea, *Amazed by Grace*, 164.

the events of their day for fifteen minutes every evening, asking themselves three questions and writing down the answers to these questions in a journal. The three questions are; 1) what surprised me today? 2) What moved me or touched me today? 3) What inspired me today? Often, these are busy people, and I tell them that they do not need to write a great deal; the key thing lies in reliving their day from a new perspective and not the amount that they write about it. Naturally, people have varying degrees of success with this process. But if they stay with it, I have seen it have a tremendous impact on a person's life. It will deepen their awareness of life, help them leave the comparison game, and lead to cultivating a grateful heart where they see everything as a gift.

Most of us lead far more meaningful lives than we know. Often, finding meaning and cultivating a grateful heart is not about doing things differently. It's about seeing familiar things in new ways. When we find new eyes, we will begin to see our many blessings in new ways. We will then find ourselves cultivating a grateful heart. We can see life in many ways: with our eyes, with our mind, with our intuition. But perhaps it is only those who have remembered to see with the heart, that life is ever deeply known or served.

"Letting go" of comparison and competition for most of us is something that requires constant awareness. It is so easy to take our eyes off our path to check out what others are doing and if they are ahead or behind us. But without comparison, concepts like *ahead* or *behind* or *best* or *worst* lose their meaning. How freeing this would be for us if we could live this way.

D. The Courage to Let Go of Achievement as the Basis of our Self Worth

When I was growing up, I somehow got the label of being "the serious one." At the time, I don't think I really understood what people meant by that, but somehow this idea of being too serious stuck with me. And conversely, because of this label, some people also thought that I didn't know how to have fun. That I needed to learn how to relax, how to play, and how to enjoy more things.

As I reflect back on these early years, I can better understand now, how people saw me in this way. And gradually, it seems to me that, without realizing it, I fell into the trap of believing that being too serious equated with being successful and being successful meant feeling good about myself. In other words, the basis of my self-worth was intimately connected to achieving. In high school, it was achieving and being very good and successful in sports. In college, it was getting good grades, so that I could get into graduate school. In graduate school, it was completing my doctorate. After my doctorate, it was getting accepted for my internships. After my internships, it was passing my licensing exams. After graduate school and passing my licensing exams, it was getting a good job that paid well. After this, it was getting my own counseling center and being accepted on the faculty of a university. As long as I was achieving, I felt good about myself.

What happened to me along the way, is that I fell into the trap of our western society that preaches the belief that your self-worth as a person is based on what you achieve, what you accomplish, and how successful you are in life.

I can also tell you that this way of thinking about myself is difficult to let go. It takes constant awareness, effort, and courage to look at this reality of my life to know there is more to who I am as a person than my successes and accomplishments. And, it takes a lot of courage to address these issues within myself and try to change them.

From my career in counseling, I have discovered that there are a lot of people like me who struggle with this idea. As I said, it is so much a part of our culture. So, in order to let go of this way of thinking and living, we need to understand that our efforts to do this are really counter-cultural. In his book, *Tuesdays with Morrie*, the author, Mitch Albom asked Morrie about how our culture tries to influence the way we think about life. Listen to what he said.

> Dying is only one thing to be sad over, Mitch. Living unhappily is something else. So many of the people who come to visit me are unhappy. Why? Because the culture we have does not make people feel good about themselves. We're teaching the wrong things. And you have to be strong enough to say if the culture doesn't work, don't buy it. Create your own. Most people can't do it. They're more unhappy than me—even in my current condition.[10]

Consequently, what we need to do to let go of this idea that our self-worth is based on our accomplishments and successes, is to realize that each of us is truly unique with certain gifts and talents that only we possess and that we are completely loved by God for who we are, and not for what we do. However, for most of us, this is easier said than done! Fortunately,

---

10. Albom, *Tuesdays with Morrie*, 35.

in my own efforts to do this, I came across an excellent book by Dr. Stuart Brown. He is a psychiatrist, clinical researcher, and founder of the National Institute for Play. In his book, *Play: How It Shapes the Brain, Opens the Imagination, and Invigorates the Soul,* Dr. Brown uses the latest advances in biology, psychology, and neurology to explain that play shapes our brain, helps us foster empathy, helps us navigate complex social groups, and is at the core of creativity and innovation. He shows us how play is essential to our health and functioning. So, what exactly is play? To begin with, Brown says that it is important to understand that play is apparently purposeless. Basically, this means that we play for the sake of play. We do it because it's fun and we want to. For most of us, in our culture, spending time doing purposeless activities is rare. In fact, for many of us, it sounds like an anxiety attack waiting to happen. We convince ourselves that playing is a waste of precious time. We've got to "get 'er done!" It doesn't matter if our job is running a multimillion-dollar company, raising a family, or finishing school, we've got to keep our noses to the grindstone and work! There's no time to play!

But Dr. Brown argues that play is not an option. In fact, he writes, "the opposite of play is not work—the opposite of play is depression. Respecting our biologically programmed need for play can transform our work. It can bring back excitement and newness to our job. Play helps us deal with difficulties and is an essential part of the creative process. Most importantly, true play that comes from our own inner needs and desires is the only path to finding lasting joy and satisfaction in our work. In the long run, work does not work without play."[11]

Coupled with this, is the similarity between our biological need for play and our body's need for rest. It seems that living and loving with our whole hearts requires us to respect our bodies' need for renewal. According to the Centers for Disease Control, insufficient sleep is associated with a number of chronic diseases and conditions, such as diabetes, heart disease, obesity, and depression. But many of us still believe that exhaustion is a status symbol of hard work and that sleep is a luxury. The result is that many of us are so very tired.

Interestingly enough, the same thoughts that tell us we're too busy to play and have fun are the ones that whisper: "one more hour of work! You can catch up on your sleep this weekend. Napping is for slackers. Push through. Keep going. You can handle it."

---

11. Brown, *Play: How It Shapes the Brain,* 32.

But the truth is, many of us over a period of time, can't handle it. We are a nation of exhausted and overstressed adults raising over scheduled children. We use our spare time to desperately search for joy and meaning in our lives. We think accomplishments, successes and achievement will bring joy and meaning, but that pursuit could be the very thing that's keeping us so tired and afraid to slow down. This is why courage is needed for us to step out into this new way of thinking and living.

If we want to "let go" of the idea that achievement, productivity and successes are the basis of our self-worth, we need to become intentional about incorporating play and rest into our daily lives. If what matters to us is what other people think or say or value, then it's back to exhaustion and producing for self-worth. Today, I think I'll choose play and rest.

E. The Courage to Let Go of the "Lone Ranger Syndrome"

When I was a youngster, my brother and I would watch several cowboy TV shows on Saturday morning. The Lone Ranger was one of our favorites. This masked man and his faithful Indian companion named Tonto would always search out the bad guys and/or come to the aid of someone in need. They always operated alone. For myself, I have come to understand this as "the Lone Ranger" syndrome.

Over the years, I have seen this way of living in many people. They feel that they have to "go it alone." To be independent, strong, and brave in the face of whatever happens to them in life. Needing to connect with others in any way is a sign of weakness.

We need to let go of this Lone Ranger syndrome, this "myth of self-sufficiency." Somehow many of us have come to equate success in life with not needing anyone. Moreover, many of us are willing to extend a helping hand to others, but we are very reluctant to reach out for help when we need it ourselves. It's as if we have divided the world into "those who offer help," and "those who need help." The truth is that we are both. Sometimes, we can even derive our self-worth from feeling like we never need help, yet always offering it.

In my experience as a psychotherapist, I have seen how this "myth of self-sufficiency," this "go it alone" syndrome has not only disconnected us from life, but for many of us, it has disconnected us from each other as well. Such qualities as self-reliance, self-determination, and self-sufficiency are so deeply admired among us that needing someone is often seen as a personal failing. A hundred and fifty years after the end of the frontier, we continue to inhabit its culture. Self-sufficiency was critically important when you lived a hundred hostile miles away from your nearest neighbor. But we can still live in this way today, even though there might be two thousand people to a city block. Needing others has come to require an act of courage. Is it so surprising that so many people are secretly lonely and afraid to grow old?

Perhaps it is this striving for excessive independence that is a weakness. Maybe this is what makes many of us so vulnerable to isolation, cynicism, and depression. But it is doubtful that this kind of independence and individualism will enable us to live in the deepest and most fulfilling way. In order to live well, we may need to know and trust one another again. To touch and be touched by those around us.

In my work, I have often found that there is a great hunger for a sense of connection and community. That below the surface of wanting to "go it alone," people really want to find others with whom they can genuinely share their lives. However, it is important to understand that this sense of loneliness, isolation, and alienation that is so prevalent in our culture is partially caused by the breakdown of the social networks that used to give us a sense of connection and community. The importance of this lies in the fact that people who feel lonely and isolated are more likely to smoke, to overeat, to abuse drugs, and work too hard. Also, many studies have shown that people who feel lonely and isolated have three to five times the risk of premature deaths, not only from heart disease but also from *all* causes when compared to those who have a sense of connection and community.

So, what is connection all about? What does it mean to feel connected to others? For me, connection is the energy that exists between people when we feel seen and heard. It is the sense we get when we feel valued and can give, receive, and share without judgment. It is what happens to us when we derive sustenance and strength from the relationship. When we understand the idea of connection in this way, it is easy for us to believe that we are "wired for connection," rather than following a "go it alone" pathway. Connection with others is in our biology. It begins with the "bonding" that we do with our mothers when we are born and develops from there as we go through life. From the time we are born, we need connection to thrive emotionally, physically, spiritually, and intellectually. A decade ago, the idea that we are "wired for connection" might have been perceived as

The Courage to "Let Go"

"touchy-feely" or New Age. Today, we know that the need for connection is more than a feeling or a hunch. It's hard science. Neuroscience, to be exact.

In his book, *Social Intelligence: The New Science of Human Relationships,* Daniel Goleman explores how the latest findings in biology and neuroscience confirm that we are hardwired for connection and that our relationships shape our biology as well as our experiences. Goleman writes, "even our most routine encounters act as regulators in the brain, priming our emotions, some desirable, others not. The more strongly connected we are with someone emotionally, the greater the mutual force."[12] It's amazing—yet perhaps not surprising—that the connectedness we experience in our relationships impacts the way our brain develops and performs.

There are many ways that we can come to feel connected to others—to feel that we belong. Sometimes, it can come to us through friendship or parenthood or work, sometimes by kindness, by compassion, by generosity or acceptance. Often, it will involve doing something for someone. These opportunities for connection can even come to us in the most unexpected ways.

Joan was a librarian who would soon be forty. She had always lived alone. Charitably speaking, Joan could be described as very, very plain. However, her sisters and her mother were truly beautiful women. When you looked at her, you could tell her clothes were not very becoming to her. She wore no jewelry or make-up and her hair was pulled back with a rubber band into a ponytail. Her finest feature was her eyes. Clear and grey, they were now filled with tears.

Life is not easy for a plain woman. From early childhood, she had felt ashamed of her looks and was painfully shy. The response of others to her simply confirmed her sense of wrongness. In school, her peers had avoided her. Her family, while loyal, were often apologetic about the way she looked. Many years before, she had simply given up. In her entire life, she had never really felt connected to anyone. She had never had an intimate relationship—never felt like she ever belonged anywhere. She felt at ease only in her home or in the library. "Librarians are invisible," she told me. She spent her days at work and her evenings in front of the TV. She had lived this way for a long time.

As her fortieth birthday grew closer, Joan became more depressed. I worried about her and began to see her more often. I offered her a place of

---

12. Goleman, *Social Intelligence,* 4–5.

acceptance and caring, but in the end it was not me, but my clients, who healed her.

As she sat in my waiting room, week after week, she began to respond to the others she saw there. Many of them were hurting like she was. She had never met people like them before, and she was surprised that she felt so comfortable with them. Although she was shy, she eventually began to speak with some of them. She had also noticed that other people often came with these clients, people who drove or shopped or helped in a variety of ways. After thinking about this for a while, she hesitantly told me that if some of my clients had no one or if their families needed an extra hand, she would be glad to help.

This was how Joan met Bill. He was a handsome thirty-two year old man who had become HIV positive about a year after his partner was diagnosed with AIDS. Bill had nursed him through his long, progressive illness and ultimate death. Slowly, he too became sick and needed help.

At first, Joan drove Bill to doctors' appointments much as she drove several others. However, most of the others had some family, but Bill was alone. As time went on, she began to shop for him and then to cook extra food at home, freeze it, and take it to him for dinner. They became friends. As things became worse, his parents had flown in to see him several times. They were older now and it had been difficult for them at first, but they were a close family and had been able to support Bill in ways that really mattered. Joan had met them too, and liked them. Like Bill, they were kind people.

Within a year, Bill became very ill. His parents had wanted him to come home but he had lived in Maryland for many years and wanted to stay there. He had applied for hospice care but discovered he was not eligible because there was no one living with him who could act as his caregiver. Many of his closest friends had already died and he had no one to turn to for help. After much prayer and reflection, Joan moved in.

Bill died in the spring. When I heard the news I called Joan because I was concerned about her and wondered if she would be able to handle things. Her depression had lifted somewhat over the past several months, but I knew Bill's death would be a great blow to her.

A few weeks later, she came to see me and told me she had been visiting Bill's parents and had attended his funeral. As she talked about the events that had led to his death, I noticed that she was wearing lipstick. When I commented on this, she looked away from me and seemed to blush.

The Courage to "Let Go"

Continuing with her story, she told me about something that had happened shortly before Bill died. He had been very weak and mostly bedridden for some time. One morning he had not been doing well, and so she called him from the library several times during the day. The hospice social worker and the nurse visited him daily and often a neighbor would look in, but as the day went on she worried about his being at home alone until she finished work.

Coming home, she had run up the stairs, her arms full of groceries. She opened the door, calling his name loudly so that he could hear her in his bedroom. But Bill was not in his bedroom. Fully dressed in a jacket, shirt and tie, he was sitting in the living room waiting for her. His clothes, still elegant, looked as if they had been bought for a much larger man, but his hair was carefully combed and he had shaved. The effort involved was hard for her to even imagine.

Stunned, she asked him why he had gotten dressed. He had looked at her for a moment. Then, he eased off the couch, and, getting down on one knee, he had asked her to marry him. She had put the groceries down then and helped him up. Hugging him for the first time, she told him how very important he was to her.

I looked at her in silence. Still blushing, she met my eye. "In my heart I did marry him you know," she told me. "He will be here with me always." Sometimes, the deepest healing comes from the natural fit between two wounded people's lives.

Joan finally felt like she belonged. She finally felt like she was connected to someone and this had a tremendous impact on her life.

This innate need we all have for connection makes the consequences of disconnection that much more real and dangerous. Sometimes, we only *think* we are connected. Technology, for instance, has become a kind of imposter for connection, making us believe we are connected when we are really not—at least not in the ways we need to be. In our technology crazed world, we have confused being communicative with feeling connected. Just because we are plugged in, doesn't mean we feel seen and heard. In fact, hyper-communication can mean we spend more time on Facebook than we do face-to-face with the people we care about. Just look around you. I can't tell you how many times I've walked into a restaurant and seen two parents on their cell phones while their kids are busy texting or playing video games. What's the point of even sitting together?

It takes courage to admit and realize that the "Lone Ranger" syndrome will not bring us happiness. But because this way of thinking and living is so embedded in our culture, it will take effort and courage on our part to realize that belonging and connection is what we all long for. This is what makes life worth living. This is what will bring us happiness. This is what Joan discovered with Bill.

F. The Courage to Let Go of Our Need to be Right

Perhaps one of the blessings of growing older is that we have a chance to gain wisdom and perspective about life. And, as I have grown older, and tried to age gracefully, I have come to realize that when life is stripped down to its very essentials, it is surprising how simple things become. Fewer and fewer things really matter, and those that do, matter a great deal more.

During my college years, Tom was one of my roommates. He was a very intelligent guy majoring in philosophy. Tom had a very forceful personality and he loved to argue—about almost anything. Basically, it didn't matter very much what the topic of discussion might be. Tom would form his opinion about the issue and would always try to prove that his point of view was right—and of course, the other person was obviously wrong. In one way, I don't know how we ever remained friends. His personality was so different from mine. Because of my family background growing up, I was always more reserved and tended to shy away from arguments and avoid conflicts as much as I could. Tom seemed to thrive on them. Maybe it was because our personalities were so different, that we somehow managed to get along fairly well. But the main thing I remember about Tom was the fact that he seemed to have this tremendous need to be right—even about minor things that truly didn't matter very much.

In my career as a psychotherapist, I have found the same dynamic occurring in the lives of many of my clients. This was especially true in the marriage counseling that I did. The need for one of the spouses to be right—and the other wrong—caused so many problems in relationships, even when the issues were not objectively very important. So often this kind of stubbornness and clinging to ideas and opinions caused so many problems and heartaches. Over time, I discovered that so many things that people argue over, don't really matter very much in the final analysis. It was just this need to be right and "win" that kept some people from being able to truly listen to their spouse and hear their point of view.

The Courage to "Let Go"

Bill and Joan were on the verge of separation when they came to see me. Even though they had been married for over twenty years, they said their relationship was filled with anger and resentment because of their constant arguing. They both agreed that they couldn't go on this way. After seeing them for several sessions, it became clear to me, and eventually to them, that many of their arguments occurred because Bill had this need to always "be right" and therefore for Joan, to always "be wrong." Of course when Joan felt that Bill was trying to prove that he was right and she was wrong about almost any issue, she would feel attacked and would fight back. It was at this point that some very heated arguments took place. This underlying dynamic in their relationship seemed to be the root cause of their constant arguments.

As we continued our work together over the next several months, it became clear to all of us why Bill had this need to always be right. It seems that he had grown up in a family where this way of thinking about who was right and who was wrong was very important. In his family, there was like a constant rivalry between his parents and siblings to "win" an argument about some issue and therefore, for someone else in the family to "lose." It didn't matter if it was a question as to who won the World Series in a particular year or who left the car lights on overnight and ran down the battery. Winning—being right—was all that mattered! His family was so consumed with this way of living, that Bill said his father actually had a coveted T-shirt emblazoned on the front with "I was Right" and on the back "You were Wrong." Everyone in the family wanted to "win" the right to wear this T-shirt.

Gradually, Bill and Joan came to understand that this all-too-human need to be right—and the corresponding need for someone else to be wrong—was seriously hurting their marriage. Over time, and with a lot of practice, they came to a point where they could begin to see when this dynamic was taking place in their conversations. Eventually, they were able to develop strategies that allowed them to break free of this win/lose dynamic. This helped them to genuinely begin to listen better to one another without arguing. Gradually, their relationship significantly improved.

Sometimes, it takes a great deal of courage and restraint *not* to say something or respond to someone else's observations or opinions about an issue. The ability to "let things go" and not feel like we have to win every argument or difference of opinion by having the last word can be very freeing in life. Years ago, as a young therapist, I spent a lot of time trying to learn how to fix life only to discover at the end of the day that life is not broken. I thought I had to have an answer for everything and needed to answer everyone's questions about who was right or wrong. How helpful it was for me to have a supervisor who had a very different approach. She helped me to understand that sometimes the best counseling approach is knowing when to say nothing at all. To put it bluntly, she told me that one of the most helpful things to learn as a therapist is when to "keep your mouth shut!" In my sessions with clients, I have often prayed for the grace to know when to do this. Through the years, I have also tried to teach the importance of this to some of my clients who always feel they have to have the last word, that they always have to be right. Sometimes, knowing when *not* to say something takes a lot of courage and restraint and is the best way to help someone.

It is very difficult to be open to another person's point of view. Especially if it is very different from our own. And, in order to do this, we have to learn to let go of our need to be right, and to realize that living life fully is much more than being right or wrong. If we could understand this, people would have fewer arguments, less hurt feelings and better relationships.

One of my clients who had a serious neurological disease told me, "before I got sick, I had this need to be right and I was certain about almost everything. I knew what I wanted and when I wanted it. Most of the time, I knew what I had to do to get it too. I walked around with my hand outstretched saying, 'I want an apple.' Many times life would give me an orange instead. But I knew what was right and what I wanted. I was always so disappointed that I never even looked at the orange to see what it was. Actually, in those days, I don't think I could have seen what it was. I had the world divided up into just two categories: 'apples' and 'not apples.' If it wasn't an apple, it was only a 'not apple.' I only had 'apple eyes.'

After living with his illness for several months, this client's way of looking at life began to gradually change. His need to be right all the time and certain about almost everything became less important to him. He came to see that life is more about living each day than winning or losing. He began to be more open to the idea that life is full of apples and oranges. And that is ok.

The willingness to win or lose—and not needing to be right all the time—moves us out of an adversarial relationship to life and into a powerful kind of openness where we can more deeply experience and participate in life. It allows us to free ourselves from win/lose thinking and the fear that feeds on it. It helps us to become free of an adversarial position toward life where we have to win and someone else has to lose.

Another client, Betty, told me an interesting story about her husband, Dave. It seems as though Dave had always been very opinionated and always needed to be right. This part of his personality had caused problems in their marriage and tended to alienate him from some family members and friends. A few years ago, Dave planned a trip for both of them to go to Hawaii. An organized and frugal man, Dave had reserved compact rental cars on each of the four islands months in advance. On arriving on the Big Island and presenting their reservation to the car rental desk, they were told that the economy car they had reserved was not available. Alarmed, Betty watched her husband's face redden as he prepared to do battle. Fortunately, the clerk did not seem to notice. "I am so sorry, sir," he said. "Will you accept a substitute for the same price? We have a mustang convertible." Barely pacified, Dave put their bags in this beautiful white sports car and they drove off.

The same thing happened throughout their holiday. They would turn in their car and fly to the next island, only to be told that the car they had been promised was not available and each time offered a same-price substitution. It was amazing, she said. After the mustang, they had been given a Mazda MR-10, a Lincoln Town Car, and finally, a Mercedes, all with the most sincere apologies and at no extra cost. Their vacation was absolutely wonderful and on the plane back, Betty turned to her husband, thanking him for all he had done to arrange such a memorable time. "Yes," he said, pleased, "it was really nice. Too bad they never had the right car for us." He was absolutely serious.

If we can learn to let go of our need to be right all the time, we will experience better relationships and more peace in our lives. It will diminish our arguments with others. It will take us out of an adversarial relationship with others where we are right and the other person is wrong. It will allow us to experience life in a new way where we can listen to the ideas and opinions of others without a need to "prove" them wrong. It will give us a better perspective in life where we realize that truly living life to the fullest is so much more than simply being right or wrong.

4

Courage and the Challenges of Life

"Everyone should be kind. Things are hard for everyone." Auggie Pullman

A. The Courage to Live with Chronic Illness

HIS DEATH SENTENCE CAME in the summer of 1994. Looking back, Morrie knew something bad was coming long before that. He knew it the day he gave up dancing.

He had always been a dancer. The music didn't matter. Rock and roll, big band, the blues. He loved them all. He used to go to a church in Harvard Square every Wednesday night for something called "Dance Free." He twisted and twirled and did the Lindy to Jimi Hendrix. No one there knew he was a prominent doctor of sociology, with years of experience as a college professor and several well-respected books. Other people there just thought he was some old nut.

But then the dancing stopped. He developed asthma in his sixties. His breathing became labored. A few years later, he began to have trouble walking. At a birthday party for a friend, he stumbled inexplicably. On another night, he fell down the steps of a theater, startling a small crowd of people. He was in his seventies by this point, so they whispered "old age" and helped him to his feet. But Morrie knew something else was wrong. This was more than old age. He was weary all the time. He had trouble sleeping. He dreamt he was dying.

He began to see doctors. Lots of them. They tested his blood. They tested his urine. Finally, when nothing could be found, one doctor ordered a muscle biopsy, taking a small piece out of his Morrie's calf. The lab report came back suggesting a neurological problem and so he had to undergo another series of tests.

Finally, on a hot, humid day in August 1994, Morrie and his wife Charlotte, went to the neurologist's office for the results. The doctor asked them to sit down before he broke the news. The doctor told Morrie that he had amyotrophic lateral sclerosis (ALS), Lou Gehrig's disease, a brutal, unforgiving illness of the neurological system. There was no known cure.

"How did I get it?" Morrie asked.

"Nobody knew."

"Is it terminal?"

"Yes."

"So, I'm going to die?"

"Yes, you are, the doctor said. I'm very sorry."[1]

As Morrie processed this news and searched for answers, the disease overtook him, day by day, week by week. He backed the car out of the garage one morning and could barely push the brakes. That was the end of his driving. He kept tripping, so he purchased a cane. This was the end of his walking free.

ALS is like a lit candle— it melts your nerves and leaves your body a pile of wax. Often, it begins with the legs and works its way up. You lose control of your thigh muscles, so you cannot support yourself standing. You lose control of your trunk muscles, so that you cannot sit up straight. By the end, if you are still alive, you are breathing through a tube in a hole in your throat, while your soul, perfectly awake, is imprisoned inside a body that no longer functions. This usually takes no more than five years from the day you contract the disease.

Morrie's doctors guessed he had two years left. Morrie knew it was less. But he had made a profound decision, one he began to construct the day he came out of the doctor's office with a sword hanging over his head. "Do I wither up and disappear, or do I make the best of my time left?" he asked himself.

---

1. Albom, *Tuesdays with Morrie*, 7.

He would not wither. He would not be ashamed of dying. Instead, he would make this illness and eventual death, the center point of his days. He would allow other people to walk this final journey with him so that he could help others understand what living through this disease was like.

Ten year old Auggie Pullman had been homeschooled his entire life because of Treacher Collins syndrome, a genetic disorder that affects a person's hearing, sight, and appearance. He loved science and wanted to go to the moon someday. Although he had twenty-seven reconstructive surgeries, he still wore a NASA space helmet everywhere to hide his face. His mom enrolled him in a prep middle school because all the sixth-graders would have been new there.

His looks startled his classmates. After his first day of class, his mother asked him, "how was your day?" "OK," Auggie replied. "The kids mostly just stared at me. The courtyard was the hardest time. During a dodge ball game, the other kids threw the ball at me and were laughing at me. Then, some of them started calling me a 'freak.'"

Soon, many of his new classmates began to tease him. One nasty bully says he'd kill himself if he looked like Auggie. Another one nicknamed him "barf hideous." Later, rumors spread that just touching him would spread the plague. Kids can be so cruel.

Auggie's illness allows us to put ourselves in someone else's shoes. Can we ever imagine the courage it would take for a child like Auggie to go to school every day—or any place for that matter—knowing that you would be stared at, teased, bullied, and made fun of?

Morrie and Auggie's experiences give us an insight and understanding into the quiet, constant, everyday courage they needed to live through each day. It gives us a glimpse into the struggles and courage of people with chronic illnesses.

And this is what I have experienced in over thirty years in my counseling work with people who have had to endure many different types of chronic illnesses or physical disabilities. I have worked with them as they have struggled to accept their illness. I have seen the courage required of them to struggle to make sense of their illness and move forward in their lives. Quite frankly, their courage has often amazed me.

The courage of people who have had to struggle with chronic illnesses or physical disabilities have taught me four important things about courage and life.

Courage and the Challenges of Life

1. *Mourning*. We might not often connect courage and mourning but the clients I have had the privilege to work with have taught me this. Every type of chronic illness or physical disability involves a loss of some kind that requires a huge adjustment on the part of the person. Sometimes, that means—like Morrie—the inability to use some part of their bodily functions. At other times, it's the loss of a person's hopes and dreams about their life. Often, there are multiple losses that require major adjustments to life on the part of the person who is afflicted by a major illness or disability. In order to move forward in their lives in some positive way, a period of mourning is often required and is the first step in the process of their healing. In *Tuesdays with Morrie*, TV personality Ted Koppel asked Morrie about how he found the courage to live each day with this illness. "Ted," he said, "when all this started, I asked myself, 'am I going to withdraw from the world, like most people do, or am I going to live?' I decided I'm going to live—or at least try to live—the way I want, with dignity, with courage, with humor, with composure. There are some mornings when I cry and cry and mourn for myself. Some mornings, I'm so angry and bitter. But it doesn't last too long. Then, I get up and say, 'I want to live'. . . . So far I've been able to do it. Will I be able to continue? I don't know. But I'm betting on myself that I will."[2]

Later on in this book, as he was reflecting on the importance of mourning, Mitch asked Morrie if he ever felt sorry for himself. "Sometimes, in the mornings," he said. "That's when I mourn. I feel around my body, I move my fingers and my hands—whatever I can still move—and I mourn what I've lost. I mourn the slow, insidious way in which I'm dying. But then I stop mourning." "Just like that?" Mitch continued. "I give myself a good cry if I need it. But then I concentrate on all the good things still in my life. On the people who are coming to see me. On the stories I'm going to hear. Mitch, I don't allow myself any more self-pity than that. A little each morning, a few tears, and that's all." Mitch thought about himself and all the people he knew who spent many of their waking hours feeling sorry for themselves. How useful it would be to put a daily limit on self-pity. Just a few tearful minutes, then on with the day. If Morrie could do it with such a horrible disease, why couldn't I?[3]

In contrast to Morrie and Auggie, Jerry was a young man with juveniles diabetes. He was diagnosed with his illness two weeks after his seventeenth

2. Ibid., 21–22.
3. Ibid., 56–57.

birthday. He responded to it with the rage of a trapped animal. Like an animal in a cage, he flung himself against the limitations of his disease, refusing to keep to a diet, forgetting to take his insulin, using his diabetes to hurt himself over and over. Fearing for his life, his parents insisted he go into therapy. He was very reluctant, but finally came.

For the first five months, we worked on Jerry's feelings about this disease, his intense anger, and how he felt it had ruined his life. Clearly, at first, he couldn't even imagine mourning what he had lost. One day, after he had been in therapy for months without making much progress, he told me that he had a dream that was so intense that he had not realized he had been asleep until he woke up.

In his dream, he found himself sitting in an empty room without a ceiling, facing a small stone statue of the Buddha. Although he was not a particularly spiritual young man, he could identify with it because in his dream, this Buddha was also a young man, not much older than himself.

He struggled to describe how the statue had looked. "It's face was very still and peaceful," he told me. But there was something more that he could not easily put into words. He fell silent, and then he told me that the Buddha seemed to be listening to something deep within himself. This statue somehow had an odd effect on Jerry. Alone in the room with it, he had felt more and more at peace himself.

He had experienced this unfamiliar sense of peace for a while when, without warning, a dagger was thrown from somewhere behind him. It buried itself deep in the Buddha's heart. Jerry was profoundly shocked. He felt betrayed, overwhelmed with feelings of despair and anguish. From the depth of these feelings had emerged a single question: "why is life like this?"

And then the statue had begun to grow, so slowly that at first he was not sure it was really happening. Suddenly, he knew beyond a doubt that this was the Buddha's response to the knife.

The statue continued to grow, its face as peaceful as before. The knife did not change either. Gradually, it became a tiny black speck on the chest of the enormous smiling Buddha. Watching this, Jerry felt something release in him and found he could breathe deeply for the first time in a long time. He woke up with tears in his eyes.

Often, when someone tells a dream, they find a deeper understanding of its meaning. As Jerry and I processed this dream, he recognized the feelings he had when he first saw the dagger. The despair and anguish, and even the question "why is life like this" were the same feelings and questions that had come up for Jerry in his doctor's office when he heard for the first time that he had diabetes. As he put it, "when this disease plunged into the heart of my life." But his response had been very different from the Buddha's.

Jerry had understood this dream like the opening of a door. When his doctors had told him that his disease was incurable, his response had been rage and despair. He had felt that the life in him had been stopped and there was no way to move forward. But in the most exquisite way possible, life had shown him something different. His dream offered him the hope of wholeness and suggested that, over time, he might grow in such a way that the wound of his illness might become a smaller and smaller part of the sum total of his life. That he might have a good life, even though it would not be an easy life. Nothing his doctors told him had suggested this possibility.

Often, people with chronic illnesses or physical disabilities become trapped, not by the force of their illness or disease, but by the power of their beliefs about it. Both of these conditions are brutal, lonely, constricting, and terrifying. But the life in us may be stronger than all that and free us even from that which we must endure. This was the way it was for Jerry. Sometimes, someone dreams a dream for all of us.

2. *Acceptance.* The second important lesson about courage and life that my clients have taught me has to do with acceptance. People with chronic illnesses or physical disabilities can't change this dimension of their lives, and therefore accepting it is often a huge struggle. In working with these clients over the years, I have had the privilege of seeing the courage these people manifest in trying to accept their situations. Just imagine the courage required to accept the reality of losing your independence and becoming almost totally dependent on someone else.

Again, in *Tuesdays with Morrie,* Morrie talks about his struggle to accept more and more of his dependence on others as this disease ravaged his body. He was in a wheelchair full-time now, trying to get used to helpers lifting him like a heavy sack from his chair to the bed and the bed to the chair. He had begun to cough while eating, and chewing was a chore. His legs were dead. He would never walk again.

Yet he refused to be depressed. "Accept what you are able to do and what you are not able to do; accept the past as past, without denying it or discarding it."[4] He struggled to accept his loss of independence bravely. Gradually, the most personal and basic things were taken from him—going

---

4. Ibid., 18.

to the bathroom, blowing his nose, and washing himself. With the exception of breathing and swallowing his food, he was dependent on others for almost everything. It was like completely surrendering to this disease.

As Morrie struggled to accept the reality of this disease as well as his growing dependence on others, Mitch asked him how he managed to stay so positive through all of this.

> Mitch, it's funny, he said. I'm an independent person, so my inclination was to fight all of this—being helped from the car, having someone else dress me. I felt a little ashamed, because our culture tells us we should be ashamed if we can't wipe our own behind. But then I figured, forget what the culture says. I have ignored the culture much of my life. I am not going to be ashamed. What's the big deal?
>
> And you know what? The strangest thing.
>
> What's that?
>
> I began to *enjoy* my dependency. Now I enjoy it when they turn me over on my side and rub cream on my behind so I don't get sores. Or when they wipe my brow, or they massage my legs. I revel in it. I close my eyes and soak it up. And it seems very familiar to me.
>
> It's like going back to being a child again. Someone to bathe you. Someone to lift you. Someone to wipe you. We all know how to be a child. It's inside all of us. For me, it's just remembering how to enjoy it.
>
> The truth is, when our mothers held us, rocked us, stroked our heads—none of us ever got enough of that. We all yearn in some way to return to those days when we were completely taken care of—unconditional love. Unconditional attention. Most of us didn't get enough. I know I didn't.[5]

In the end, Morrie's struggle to accept his situation and the courage it took to do this gave him a sense of peace and contentment.

3. *Endurance.* The third dimension of life that the courage of the chronically ill or physically disabled person exemplified for me was endurance. My clients have shown me how important endurance is for them—and for all of us. It's one thing to have to endure something for a short or even specific period of time. But it's quite another thing to be chronically ill or physically disabled and have to endure a situation for many years—perhaps

---

5. Ibid., 116.

for one's entire life. This takes a tremendous amount of courage each and every day.

Although he is largely incapacitated now and can't speak without the aid of a computerized voice, O.J. Brigance knows his life has value. This former Baltimore Ravens football linebacker offers a message of hope to others by the way he lives his life and patiently endures this devastating illness. "Every day, every hour, every minute, every second of life, is God-given and valuable," he said.

When Brigance was diagnosed eight years ago with ALS, the news was daunting for both himself and his wife. It took him many months to grieve and accept his illness and to realize that he would have to endure this new reality for the rest of his life. "Once we grieved, we came to the decision that adverse circumstances in no way delete purpose or destiny in one's life," he said. "Have there been days where it has been challenging? Of course. However, I did not create my life, so I have no right to negate my life."[6]

Brigance emphasized that because he decided to live the best he could after his diagnosis, there has been a ripple effect of goodness in the world. In 2008, he and his wife, Chanda, created the Brigance Brigade Foundation to encourage and empower those living with ALS. Although he can't use his hands anymore, he was even able to write a book several years ago. He currently serves as Senior Advisor to Player Engagement for the Baltimore Ravens. Through his courage and patient endurance, he has been able to give of himself and encourage people who struggle with all kinds of illnesses.

Brigance shows us that whatever we are called upon to endure in life requires courage and can certainly be a way that we can bring goodness into our world. And, if we can endure it with patience and without resentment, it will bring healing to many others.

4. *Vulnerability.* David Watson says that his own thinking about vulnerability has been shaped by his son Sean. He is eight years old. He has a body that is different from most other bodies. He has an extra copy of the twenty-first chromosome in every cell of his body. This means that his brain works differently than is "typical." It is harder for him to learn some things. He has matured, intellectually and emotionally, more slowly than other children his age. He is said to be "delayed." He is "behind" other eight-year-olds, they say. He is subject to various clinical diagnoses: Downs syndrome or tresome 21. He has features described as "phenotypical": a slight upward turn to his eyes, a small nose and small ears, and a bit of a

---

6. https://www.amazon.com/strength-champion-finding-fortitude.

gap between his first and second toes. He also has a large scar across his chest from open heart surgery at four months of age. Most people cannot understand his speech, although he talks all the time.[7]

Sean is the most vulnerable member of his family. He often does not understand that the world around him can and will hurt him. Left to his own devices, he might walk out into the middle of the street, grab a hot pan on the stove, or hug someone who might misunderstand his intentions. People like Sean are not highly valued by the world. People with Downs syndrome are often the butt of jokes, and it is difficult for them to advocate for themselves.

It is not coincidental that Sean's dominant personality traits are friendliness, openness, and the ability to love. Traits like these are often attributed to people with Down syndrome. Sean is so loving because he feels so little need to hide himself from others. It is not uncommon for people with Down syndrome to have a less defensive posture than "typical" people do. By their very vulnerability, they make themselves more available for relationships with—and rejection by—the rest of us.

Vulnerability allows us to genuinely connect with one another. But many of us are afraid to let our true selves be seen and known. It takes a great deal of courage to allow our true selves to be seen and known by another. Most of us spend a great deal of time and emotional energy trying to protect our true selves from being seen. We wear our masks, always trying to act or say the right things so that we can "fit in" and impress others. We all struggle with shame and the fear of "not being enough." It takes a great deal of courage to "let go" of who you think you are supposed to be and embrace who you are. For many of us, it takes courage to worry less about "what people might think," to let go of our need to please, perform and be perfect. It takes courage to be vulnerable, to be honest with ourselves, to be open to new ideas, new ways of thinking about things, or new questions that might open up new possibilities in our lives.

It is also very difficult to share our weaknesses. Asking for help as well as accepting and receiving care from someone else when we need it can be extremely challenging for many of us. In our society, it is often seen as a sign of weakness. We are supposed to be strong. We are supposed to take care of ourselves. In my counseling practice, I saw these beliefs lived out in the lives of so many people—especially men. Our culture teaches men to believe in so many ways that it is "unmanly" to ask for help and that you

---

7. Watson, "Embodiment, Vulnerability, and Relationships," 23.

are weak if you say you have needs. And so, men often will not share their weakness with anyone. However, they often pay the price for this in their own personal lives and relationships.

Allowing ourselves to receive care from others makes us vulnerable. Many people fear being vulnerable because this can open us up to being hurt and people try to protect themselves from being hurt at all costs. However, at the heart of any real intimacy is a certain vulnerability. It is difficult to trust someone with your vulnerability unless you know that they truly care for you and that you will not be judged. Rather than protecting ourselves from being hurt, it is really our imperfections and even our pain that can draw us closer to others.

Retreats are often experiences where participants allow themselves to be vulnerable and open themselves to painful memories because a bond of trust develops among the retreatants. Some years ago, I participated in a men's retreat and in one of our sessions, we were asked to find something that symbolized what was important to us at this time in our lives. Then, we all came together to share the meaning of our symbols with each other.

In our sharing session, one of the retreatants said that his symbol was not an object but rather he was remembering a part of Beethoven's Ninth Symphony with its extraordinary "Ode to Joy." He reminded us that Beethoven had written his Ninth Symphony when he was totally deaf. When I asked him why he chose this as his symbol, he said he was not sure. Maybe others could be helped to overcome their limitations or disabilities in the same way.

Although this seemed reasonable enough, I suspected that there might be more to it than this. Deciding to pursue it a little, I asked him where he had last heard Beethoven's Ninth. He looked at me steadily and his eyes became sad. It had been played four weeks ago at the memorial service of his friend who had died in a motorcycle accident. The reteatants became very quiet. "What have you learned from your friend's death?" I asked him. He paused and thought for a moment. He missed his friend terribly, he told us. Several times in these past weeks, he had reached for the phone to call him and share something with him. Each time he felt his loss more deeply. He had tried talking to others but it had not been the same. It never would be. He had not thought about it in so many words, but his friend's death had shown him that no one can be replaced. "Every life is unique and precious," he said. "I guess this is the bottom line for me. If this wasn't the case, all this other stuff we have been talking about wouldn't matter to me at all." We all sat together thinking this over. In the silence, many of us recognized that this was the bottom line for us too. This person allowed himself to be vulnerable because a bond of trust had developed among this group of men.

It is interesting to note that in the movie *Wonder,* Auggie Pullman had shown a tremendous amount of vulnerability and courage in facing each day with his illness as he went to school knowing that he would be teased, called many derogatory names, bullied and made fun of. Yet, somehow he could still remain positive. "Everyone should be kind," he said. "Things are hard for everyone."

B. The Courage of People Struggling with Mental Illness

One night in the emergency room, a young woman was brought in comatose, having taken a massive dose of prescription drugs. Shortly after she arrived, her heart had stopped. The ER staff worked to resuscitate her for some time, not because they had much hope of success but because they knew it was important to those who survive to feel that everything possible had been done. They had not been successful. It fell to the physician who had led the Code Team to tell her husband that his wife had died. Despite the pressures of the busy emergency room, he had sat with this man for quite a while and listened to his story.

He and his wife had not lived in Maryland very long. They were both children of violent and alcoholic families, and they had moved east with the hope of making something better for themselves. He was a mechanic; she waited tables in a bar. All they owned was a small home, a truck and his tools. A week ago, the tools had been stolen and there was no money to replace them.

Neither of them were very strong emotionally. He had often been depressed and told the doctor that when his moods came on him, they would drive to the beach and he would sit next to the ocean for hours. She would wait in the truck, watching, to be sure that he did not go too far. She had suffered from depression also. Sometimes, she would wake up in the night and wander through their little place, and he would always hear her and awaken to sit with her in the dark. They were all each other had. But this night, he had not heard her awaken. She had gone to the medicine cabinet and taken down the bottle of Elavil she had been given at the mental health clinic the week before. In it was a four month supply of pills. She had swallowed them all. He thanked the doctor for his efforts. It had been too many pills, too much pain, many years too late to bring her back. Once again the doctor assured him that everything possible had been done. The man had sat quietly thinking it over. "Everything possible had been done," he said, nodding. "Everything."

The doctor was deeply moved by the simplicity of this man's life and the depth of his love for his wife. His heart went out to him in his loss. He had been a devoted husband. But she had been mortally wounded long before she had been loved so completely.

On several occasions over the next few days, this doctor found himself thinking about this man and his wife. There in the waiting room, he had sensed in him a sort of acceptance that was puzzling. He was young, and it had never occurred to him that some pain might be beyond the power of love to heal. He had found that thought humbling. Is that what this husband had known? Is that what he had accepted? If so, how had he found the courage to love her so completely? And having loved her in this way, how could he go on?

About a month later, on another busy night in the ER, one of the nurses came to tell this same doctor that a man whose wife had been seen the month before was waiting to speak with him. She did not know the man's name, and, certain that he would not remember the details of the case, he had asked the nurse to get the wife's chart before he went to see what was needed. But by the time the chart was found, the man had gone. He had left a message. "Tell the doctor she is healed and in heaven now," he had said.

The doctor had been touched and puzzled by this message. However, four years later in the anguished aftermath of his own wife's suicide, surrounded by many well-intentioned and important words of comfort, it was this man whose words he had remembered. "He understood the power of acceptance," the man had told the doctor. "It is the only way for those who survive to find peace and heal. I think in time I will be able to go on because I know that I could not have loved her more. No one could have. But she had been wounded long ago, long before I ever knew her name. The man in the emergency room, he would have understood."

In over thirty years in working as a psychotherapist, I have come to understand that we can never know the internal struggles and anguish of another person. Over the years, I have worked with many people who struggle with the constant, quiet, ongoing pain of mental illness. Their courage and spirit of resilience has amazed me. These people are certainly a hidden face of courage.

We know that mental illness is no "respecter of persons." There are literally millions of people in the U.S. who battle this illness every day of their lives. Anyone—young and old, famous people or ordinary folks, rich or poor, can struggle with a variety of mental problems. Take well known ABC *Good Morning America* meteorologist Ginger Zee who recently shared her battle with depression in *People* magazine. She said when she was 21, she locked herself in her bathroom and took every pill she could find in her medicine cabinet. "I'd lost all hope," she said. She had just graduated from Valparaiso University in Indiana and was struggling to find her footing. "My career did not kick off in the way that I expected it to—no one wanted me on TV," she said. In an unexplainable moment, her brain told her to kill herself. "I just shut down. It wasn't worth living. I was wasting people's time and space." Fortunately, her roommate realized what she had done and got her to the hospital. Luckily, the concoction she had taken wasn't lethal. She was diagnosed with depression. "It's scary, the way your mind can overpower what is real and what is right," she said. "Now, as a mother, to think that could be my child. That is frightening."

Ginger Zee describes her struggles with mental illness in her new book *Natural Disaster: I Cover Them. I Am One*. She describes her upbringing in Grand Rapids, Michigan as somewhat "chaotic." When she was seven, her parents divorced, and she developed severe anorexia in an attempt to maintain some control. "It really went far, and it was a scary time in my life," she says. With the help of her mother, she fought this mental health issue with intensive therapy.

Now, she says there are still days when she questions herself, but she says becoming a mom has given her new strength and perspective. She hopes that being candid about her mental health struggles will spark a national dialogue. "We should treat each other with love and respect," she says, "because that glossy image you see is never the person that's really inside there."[8]

When I was young, probably about ten or eleven, I remember playing with Skipper, a neighborhood friend. Sometimes, we would play at his house. At other times, my house. When we would go to his house, I remember that his mother often seemed to act strangely and I didn't understand why. I just thought she was a very moody person. Sometimes, she would be

---

8. Zee, *Natural Disaster: I Cover Them. I Am One.*

very friendly, interacting with us in a very pleasant way. At other times, she seemed to be extremely agitated and angry, often yelling at us and telling us to go home. Being a youngster, I couldn't understand why her moods seemed to change so dramatically.

Many years later, when I was in college, one of my friends was Bob. Basically, he was an artist and pursuing an arts degree. He was especially good at pottery and made some beautiful pieces that he sold in order to help pay his way through college. On some occasions, whenever there was an arts and craft show coming up, I wouldn't see Bob for several days. When I ask him about this, he said that he was making his pieces of pottery for the show. He literally would stay awake for two or three days, working around the clock. He said he felt full of energy, like he was "on top of the world." Then, after the show, he would "crash," and again, I wouldn't see him for two or three days. He said he was catching up on his sleep. But I also noticed that when he emerged, he seemed to be "down"—almost depressed for a few days. This type of cycle continued for the duration of our college years. At the time, Bob's behavior seemed very strange to me, but he told me it "worked for him."

Several years later when I was in graduate school studying psychology, I came to understand that Skipper's mother and Bob probably suffered from bipolar disorder. This disorder, which stems from a chemical imbalance in the brain, can be very difficult to treat. However, in recent years, some new medicines have been developed that can be extremely helpful in leveling out the moods of people who suffer from this mental illness. Before that, intensive therapy could be helpful, but these new medicines helped people feel better and function better in a shorter amount of time. The bipolar clients that I worked with over the years, always showed great day to day courage trying to manage their mood swings so that this illness didn't impact their daily routines in some negative ways.

Another mental health illness which requires courage to live every day is schizophrenia. Tom was one of my clients who suffered from this illness. He was in his forties when I began to work with him but he had suffered from this illness since his early twenties. He had a mental breakdown at this time in college, and was hospitalized to stabilize him. Since then, he was put on heavy doses of medication and needed to live with his father for supervision. He disliked both of these ideas a great deal. Moreover, because of this illness, he was unable to work which was also very frustrating for him.

When Tom came for his appointments, he was ofter unshaven and disheveled. Sometimes, his speech was slurred and he had difficultly in making himself understood. My heart went out to him. He tried so hard and even thought about trying to write about his story as a way of trying to help others. Unfortunately, this never happened.

Two areas of Tom's life were particularly challenging to him as well as myself and had a huge impact on his life. The first was taking his medicine. Although he realized that it helped his moods and behavior, he hated taking them because of their significant side effects. Working with his psychiatrist, we tried numerous medications which helped to some degree but could never find one that had little or no significant side effects. Then, whenever Tom would get fed up with the ways these medicines made him feel, he would stop taking them. At that point, his behavior could become very bizarre and at times he had to be found by the police.

The second area of Tom's life that he constantly struggled with was living at home with his Dad. He was in his forties now, and wanted to be out on his own—having his own place. Over the course of several years, he was able to try this twice. On one occasion, he tried living in a group home for people with mental illness but disliked this more than living at home. On another occasion, he moved out and rented an apartment. At first, this worked out pretty well, but after several months, he would stop taking his medications, and relapse. He then had to move back in with his father.

Schizophrenia is a very difficult mental illness to treat. Although the medications have improved in recent years, they can still have significant side effects which can make it very difficult for the person. Nevertheless, I saw Tom manifest a tremendous amount of courage in our time of working together. Can you imagine how difficult it can be for some people with this illness to do the simplest of things every day that we take for granted? Things like remembering to follow a simple schedule, getting yourself dressed properly and taking care of your bodily needs, going to work each day, making friends, enjoying social events. This illness often makes a person feel extremely isolated and alone. Friendships and/or relationships are difficult to cultivate and maintain. But I saw Tom try to deal with these—and many other issues—on a daily basis with tremendous courage. It was always very inspiring to me.

Anorexia and bulimia are also mental health issues that can have tremendous repercussions for a person. They often impact the physical well being of an individual. But at the same time, people who struggle with this illness can still help others in ways they might not realize at the time. It's almost like their courage shines through them.

When Emily became ill many years ago, bulimia was not yet a household word. Filled with guilt at her uncontrollable behavior, she had been taken to specialist after specialist until finally a doctor was able to identify the problem as something more than teenage rebellion. Her illness had been so severe that she had been hospitalized for a year. This had literally saved her life. Slowly, she fought her way back from the edge, surrounded by concerned and loving adults who could not understand why she was bringing this on herself. Emily did not understand it either.

As she described it to me: "I just felt so *alone*, I could not stop myself and at the worst of it I was not sure that it was possible to survive this. I was very afraid. I remember thinking that somewhere there must be someone else who has this problem, someone who has been able to heal from it. If they could, maybe I could too." At the time, Emily did not meet another person with bulimia, but after many years of difficultly, she had somehow found her own way through this illness and was able to recover. She could not really explain why.

A few years ago, she was reading her evening newspaper and came across an announcement for a meeting of a bulimia support group. Emily was a middle-aged woman now and had not suffered from this problem for many years, but the idea of a support group intrigued her, and so she decided to attend a meeting to see what it was like. It had been a powerful experience. The desperately ill young people there had touched her heart and although she felt unable to help them, she cared about them and continued going back. Other than saying she had bulimia as a girl, she had not revealed a great deal more about herself but had simply sat and listened to the stories of the others.

As she was about to leave one of these meetings, she was stopped by a painfully thin young girl who thanked her for coming to the meetings and told her how much it had meant to know her. The girl's eyes had been filled with tears. Emily responded with her usual graciousness, but she had been puzzled. She could not recall ever speaking to this girl and did not even know her name. As she drove home, she wondered how she could have forgotten something so important to someone else. She was almost home before she understood. Her husband, who met her at the front door, was surprised to see that she had been crying. "Emily, what is wrong?" he asked. "I have become the person I needed to meet, Harry," she told him as she walked into the house.

Sometimes, our presence shines through us, even when we are not aware of it. We become a healing presence to others simply by being who we are.

Anorexia and bulimia disorders are often very confusing and complicated. For those of us who have never struggled with these issues, we can wonder, "why is this person starving themselves? Why don't they just eat?" Or, "why doesn't this person who is bulimic just stop throwing up?" I often ran into these ideas with the families and friends of the person who was ill. But, like most things, it is difficult to understand if we are not afflicted with this illness. And yet, I have often been amazed to witness the courage of these people. The courage to eat—and gain weight—when you are deathly afraid of this. The courage of the person with bulimia, desperately trying to eat—and not throw up. This kind of effort demanded a kind of courage that most of us never experience.

Everyone has been wounded in life. It is the wisdom gained from our wounds and from our own experiences of suffering that makes us able to heal. Becoming an expert is less important than remembering and trusting the wholeness in myself and everyone else. Expertise might cure, but wounded people can best be healed by other wounded people, like Emily. Only other wounded people can understand the courage that is needed, because the healing of suffering is compassion, not expertise.

C. The Courage of the Poor

A few years ago, I had the privilege of driving my daughter to high school. It was a special time for me—and, I hope for her. It gave us time to talk about many important teenage topics and led to many interesting discussions.

Because we had to go through downtown Baltimore, we often stopped at traffic lights where people would be begging—for food, shelter, money, possibly a job. These people would walk among the cars with their signs in hand. Rarely would they ever say a word, unless we said something first. My daughter was often upset by the plight of these people and she wondered not only why so many people were poor but could we do anything to help them. After discussing several possibilities, we decided to pack a lunch for them and give it to people as we stopped at a red light.

After doing this for a while, I began to think of other ways to try and help the poor. I knew there was a place in downtown Baltimore called the Franciscan Center and decided to call and see if I could volunteer to help in some way. After going for an interview, I was shown around the Center and discovered that they fed lunch five days a week to over three hundred people each day, distributed clothing, helped people write resumes and look for a job, and helped with emergency financial aid. At the close of the interview process, I told the person that I would like to volunteer to work in the soup kitchen.

The first time I went, I met the kitchen manager and asked him what I could do to help. "Stand here," he said, as he gave me an apron and a pair of gloves. "Prepare the bread for our guests." For about the next two hours, I sliced and buttered more than three hundred rolls. Then a sudden quiet came over the dining room. I looked toward the kitchen and saw a line of volunteers setting out steaming pans. Our kitchen manager came out and nodded. "It's time." He removed the sign that was blocking the entrance way, and people began slowly filing into the room in an orderly single file that would speed the path to lunch. A hand was raised and quiet again settled over the room, followed by a brief prayer of thanks.

For the next two years, I went to the Franciscan Center on most Wednesdays to feed the poor. After several weeks, I noticed that many of the same people came every Wednesday. It gave me a chance to get to know some of them. People of all ages, entire families, children, teenagers, the elderly, all came with grateful hearts. Our guests, the forgotten and the outcasts, came to the dining room not only for a meal, but also to be seen, to be remembered, to be loved as Christ. One gentleman came through the line constantly talking out loud, as if to keep an evil spirit away. An elderly lady who was very cross-eyed, tried to look directly at me to say thanks. A transgendered person picked up her food quickly and kept moving. One lady's voice was hoarse and her nails ragged. She was dressed in very worn out clothes. Another man, probably in his thirties, carried with him a stuffed animal to which he spoke in a language known only to him and to God. As I watched this gentleman, I wondered how many people have looked away from this young man? How many have looked away from his pain? Somehow, my heart ached for this young man because I could not have a conversation with him. His mind was occupied. So, I smiled, said hello, and whispered a prayer for him.

In that safe and welcoming space, this man could be himself and be seen. Nothing was required. I could try to listen with my heart even though I knew he wouldn't talk to me. I could look at him with reverence and offer a silent prayer that he would be safe when he left the sanctuary of the dining room and returned to a world that is not always friendly to those who are different from what most people consider to be normal.

In the Gospels, we see that Jesus welcomed the poor and loved every person who was perceived to be a stranger, an outsider, or someone who might be different. He welcomed Nicodemus, a Pharisee and a leading Jew, who came to Him at night because he was afraid to come for a conversation during the day (Jn 3: 1). He stopped to talk with Zacchaeus as he walked through the town of Jericho. Zacchaeus was a senior tax collector and a wealthy man but he was also short and couldn't see Jesus because of the crowd. So, he ran ahead and climbed up a sycamore tree to catch a glimpse of Jesus. When Jesus saw him up in the tree, He greeted him and told him to come down because he was going to go to his house that day (Luke 19: 1–6). It must have taken both of these men a great deal of courage to break with their Jewish and societal traditions and their roles as a leading Jew and a despised tax collector. Furthermore, Jesus always seemed to have a soft spot for the marginal people in life, those who were considered to be outcasts of society. He touched, healed and blessed them. In fact, he spoke highly of a beggar named Lazarus who lay under a rich man's table, begging for crumbs (Luke 16: 19–31). We are meant to do the same, because it is through our encounters with other people, some of whom are very different than us, that our hearts expand and we can fulfill the greatest command: to love one another. In the soup kitchen, this love was not abstract. It was concrete. Right there in front of us. I tried to love this particular person standing in front of me. I tried to physically show my love with a smile and a warm meal.

After I had been at the Center for several months, I was assigned to serve desserts. I enjoyed this very much, not only because I like desserts, but because we always had three or four desserts to choose from and it was so nice to see our guest's faces light up as they tried to decide which one to choose. I smiled at a gentleman and asked, "what would you like?" Another woman shook her head, waved a hand as if to brush aside me and the desserts, and perhaps the entire dining room. Another person asked for extra dessert for her friend who was sitting in a wheelchair at the end of the table.

COURAGE AND THE CHALLENGES OF LIFE

During the years that I worked at the Franciscan Center, I must admit that I sometimes asked myself why I was doing this. In the long run, what difference is this going to make for so many poor people who suffer every day with overwhelming sorrows and challenges? Then I remember two things. The first is what Jesus told his disciples in Matthew's Gospel: "For I was hungry and you gave me food; I was thirsty and you gave me drink; I was a stranger and you made me welcome; naked and you clothed me, sick and you visited me, in prison and you came to see me. . . . I tell you solemnly, in so far as you did this to one of the least of these brothers of mine, you did it to me" (Matt 25: 35–40).

The second thing I remember is a story about a starfish. It seems as though there was an elderly man who used to walk along the beach at low tide, picking up starfish drying in the sun and gently throwing them back into the ocean. He had been doing this for some time when a jogger overtook him and asked him what he was doing. The old man explained that the starfish would die in the sun, and so he was throwing them back into the ocean. Astounded, the younger man began to laugh. "Why, old fellow, don't waste your time. Can't you see that there are hundreds and hundreds of starfish on this beach? And thousands of beaches in this world? And another low tide tomorrow? What makes you think you can make a difference?" Still laughing, he ran on down the beach.

The old man watched him for a long time. Then he walked on and before long he passed another starfish. Stooping, he picked it up, looked at it thoughtfully and smiled. Then, gently, he threw it back into the ocean. "Made a difference to that one," he said to himself.

Sometimes, we can become so caught up in and overwhelmed by the problems in our world, our society and our communities that we don't remember that our work is not about changing society—a world we cannot completely change. Rather, it's about touching the lives that touch mine in a way that makes a difference. The Dalai Lama has said that "compassion occurs only between equals." For those who have compassion, woundedness is not a place of judgment but a place of genuine meeting.

We have moved away from the Baltimore area, so I no longer have the opportunity to volunteer at the Franciscan Center. I miss that. I miss the opportunity of not only serving the poor but learning from them as well. I must admit that before my experience of volunteering at the Franciscan Center, I did not think very much about the courage of the poor. However, as I reflect on my time there, I remember listening to the stories of men and women that exemplified a tremendously courageous spirit. The courage that was needed on some days for them just to get out of bed. The many stories of others talking about the courage and perseverance it took to navigate the various agencies that are supposed to help them in some way. The courage of Joan, a single mom, trying to raise her two small children, by working two jobs and finding it hard to make ends meet. The courage of Joe, who was fighting an alcohol addiction each minute of every day and trying now to go to at least two AA meetings every day. The courage of an elderly couple trying to learn how to live on their meager social security income and trying to complete the maze of paperwork to apply for disability benefits. The courage of Sam, a teenager, who was being parented by a single dad who was addicted to heroin, and determined to do whatever it took to stay in high school and make something of himself. These stories, and so many others, gave me new insight into the courage of the poor.

In the soup kitchen and dining room of the Franciscan Center, I began to understand what Sara Miles, an Episcopal pastor in San Francisco, described in her book, *Jesus Freak*, when she talked about our call to be healers. "Jesus calls his disciples, giving us authority to heal and sending us out. . . . He doesn't show us how to make a blind man see, dry every tear, or even drive out all kinds of demons. But he shows us how to enter into a way of life in which the broken and sick pieces are held in love, and given meaning."[9] For me, after my experience in the soup kitchen, her framing of discipleship in this way made complete sense.

In the dining room of the Franciscan Center, a new understanding of the healing work of Jesus began to grow in me. As Sara Miles writes, "I knew to the extent that new life was real, in any of us, it had sprung, just as Jesus promised, from actual feeding, healing, and forgiving. It didn't come from the sky, but from plates of enchiladas, the bruises of strangers, frustration and tears."[10] It flourishes in the freedom of knowing we do not have to hide our wounds. In the dining room, we became one body, repairing one another's torn hearts, sometimes with a hot meal, a sandwich, and a cup of coffee, sometimes with a kind word, always with our presence.

---

9. Miles, *Jesus Freak*, 105.
10. Ibid., 127–28.

D. The Courage to Live a Chaste Life

St. Augustine (354–430), as we know, had two conversions, one in his head and the other in his heart. At age twenty-five, he converted to Christianity, at least intellectually. After years of experimenting with various pagan philosophies and ways of living, he was now convinced in his head that Christianity was correct. The rest of him, however, was not so sure. For nine more years, until he was thirty-four years old, he was unable to bring his moral life into harmony with his intellectual faith. It was during these years that he frequently prayed his infamous prayer: "Lord, make me a good and chaste Christian but not yet."

Some years ago, I was working with a young nun who was trying to discern whether to stay in religions life or not. Her struggle was not easy. On the one hand, she believed that she was being called to be a nun, even though the vows of poverty, chastity, and obedience were difficult for her. On the other hand, she had been growing more and more restless over the past year and found convent life extremely challenging.

Eventually, she made the decision to leave. Her reasoning and words are echoed by many people in our culture as they try to sort out their spiritual lives. "I've decided that I am too full of life to ever be truly religious," she said. "I love life too much, am too sexual, too physical, too red-blooded, and too much rooted in this earth and what it offers to ever be really spiritual. I can't serve God and the church. I've too much erotic and creative energy."

What this nun articulates here is the divorce in Western culture between religion and eros. Like all divorces, it was painful, and as in all divorces, the property got divided up. Religion got to keep God and the secular got to keep sex. The secular got passion and God got chastity.

In our Western culture, religion, especially as it is lived out in our churches, is perceived as being anti-erotic, anti-sex, anti-creative, anti-enjoyment, and anti-this-world. The God who underwrites the churches is then perceived as stoic, celibate, dull, otherworldly, threatened by sex and by human creativity. The secular world is seen as the champion of eros, sex, creativity, and enjoyment, but is also seen as anti-God and anti-church. And so, the question arises, how can we pick between the two?

Fortunately, for most of us, we don't have to decide about keeping vows of poverty, chastity, and obedience. But all of us are invited to live chaste lives. But what does that mean?

We don't hear or read very much about this idea of chastity anymore. For many people, living this way is certainly counter-cultural and requires a tremendous amount of courage to go "against the grain," so to speak. Except for people in religious life who take the vow of chastity, the term is rarely mentioned. This is unfortunate. There is a richness to this concept that can add a wonderful dimension to our spiritual and psychological lives. However, for many people in our secular society, to live a chaste life is to be bound to the past, to be unenlightened, to be "out of touch," and to not really understand the modern world.

For a Christian, sex always needs the protection of a healthy chastity. In the Christian view of things, chastity is one of the keys to a healthy sexuality. This, however, needs to be correctly understood. So, what is chastity all about and what does having the courage to live a chaste life do to our lives?

First, there is the concept of chastity itself. Chastity is not the same thing as celibacy. To be chaste does not mean that one does not have sex. Nor does it mean that one is a prude. Basically, chastity is not even primarily a sexual concept, although faults in chastity are often within the area of sexuality.

Chastity has to do with how we experience everything. It's about the appropriateness of any experience. Ultimately, chastity is reverence—and sin, all sin, is irreverence. To be chaste is to experience people, things, places, entertainment, the phases of our lives, and sex respectfully, in a way that does not violate them or ourselves. To be chaste is to experience things reverently, in such a way that the experience leaves both them and ourselves more, not less, integrated.

Therefore, we are chaste when we relate to others in a way that does not transgress their moral, psychological, emotional, aesthetic, and sexual boundaries. That is an abstract way of saying that we are chaste when we do not let irreverence or selfishness ruin what is a gift by somehow violating it. Conversely, we lack chastity when we cross boundaries prematurely or irreverently, when we violate anyone or anything in any way, and somehow reduce what it is. Chastity is respect and reverence. Its fruits are integration, gratitude, and joy. Lack of chastity is irreverence and violation. Its fruits are bitterness and cynicism. Wherever there is violence, disrespect, emotional chaos, lack of community, bitterness, cynicism, and sexual irresponsibility, there is lack of chastity.

Courage and the Challenges of Life

Sex, precisely because it is such a powerful force within us, always needs the protection of chastity. As Carl Jung suggests, we should never be naive about the power of these energetic forces. All energy, especially sexual energy, is not always friendly and it often seeks to take us across borders and boundaries in an irreverent way. This is why there is more than a little wisdom in some of the classical ideas about sex. Sexual energy can be so powerful and sacred that it needs to be disciplined and contained by more things than just our emotional state on a given day. This wisdom of the ages, some codified in the commandments and some buried archetypically in our instincts, tells us that, before the energy of sex, we should stand in a certain reverence and holy awe, knowing that divine energy demands that we take off our shoes (Exod 3: 1–6).

However, our Western culture today vehemently disagrees with these ideas. Few things are as subject to cynicism today as is the concept of sexual chastity. Our contemporary culture considers the overcoming of chastity a moral victory. Again, this is why living a chaste life is so counter-cultural. Finally, they say, we have been set free sexually. Yet, look at our situation today. Promiscuous behavior is rampant; people are treated as objects to be used for selfish needs and one's enjoyment; teenagers engage in sexual behavior at early ages; because of the internet, pornography is engaged in by more people than ever; traditional marriage is at an all time low while people living together is at an all time high. This is where our so called enlightened age has led us. In this milieu, no wonder the idea of chastity is laughed at. However, it is interesting to note that this sexual liberation has not translated into more respect and reverence between the sexes. It hasn't resulted in less sexual exploitation of others, or helped people create a society of less lonely, more loving, more gracious and happier adults. Sadly, this is not the case and one is reminded of Albert Camus' lament that there is a time when moving beyond chastity is considered a victory, but this soon turns into a defeat.[11]

In this milieu, chastity seems outdated, old fashioned and irrelevant. It then becomes easy to dismiss the idea that the person who chooses to live chastely as being out of step, "out of touch," with modern society. This is why courage is required to lead a chaste life. Living chastely today is so counter cultural. When we try to live in this way, we are taking on so many prevalent ideas that many people live by. In order to live in this way in our culture, not only does it require a great deal of courage but we need the

---

11. Quoted by Oliver Todd, in *Albert Camus, A Life*, 157.

support of others. We need a community that we can belong to that will give us the strength to persevere in this way of life. Someone once said that Christianity does not understand sexual passion while the world does not understand chastity. Although this might be an oversimplification, it nevertheless remains true as a generalization and says something very important. Christianity has struggled, and still does, to fully celebrate sexual passion in a healthy way. The world, for its part, has struggled, and still does, to honestly and courageously look at what happens to our innocence and our happiness when we denigrate chastity. Both need to learn from each other. Passion and chastity, sex and purity, must be brought together.

Christianity must have the courage to let go of some of its fears and timidities and learn to celebrate the goodness of sex. As long as it hesitates to do this, it will, at this level at least, remain the enemy of legitimate delight and creativity. On the other hand, our culture must relearn the value of chastity and purity. It must admit how much of its emotional pain and chaos is the result of trivializing sex and ignoring the value of chastity and purity. It must understand the importance of treating everyone and everything with reverence. As long as the world continues to see chastity as naivete, fear, and Victorian morality, it will remain its own enemy. Sexual passion is only something of depth when it is related to chastity and purity.

E. The Courage to Give "The More"

There is an interesting story about a prince and a beggar. Every day a very wealthy prince would ride in his ornate carriage through the countryside. And each day he would pass a poor beggar sitting along the side of the road. Whenever the prince saw the beggar, he would stop and walk over to the beggar. As he approached, the beggar would hold out his hand and the prince would give him several coins. Then they would both go on their way. One day, as they passed each other, the prince stopped and as the beggar approached him, the prince held out his hand to the beggar first. So, the beggar reached into his little purse, took out a grain of corn and placed it in the hand of the prince. Then they both went on their way. A little while later, the beggar stopped to rest along the side of the road. He opened his purse and discovered to his amazement that in place of the grain of corn that he had given to the prince, there was a piece of gold. Then, the beggar began to cry because he wished that he had given all his pieces of corn to the prince!

So often in life, we are like the beggar trusting in the goodness of the prince—the Lord. We approach Him with outstretched hands for so many things and because of his love for us, He takes care of us. But sometimes, just like the prince, the Lord offers his hand to us first. It is then that we are invited to take something out of our bag of life, to become more generous, and put it in the hand of the Lord. We are invited to trust Him more deeply, because no matter what happens to us in life, He is there for us. We are invited to take our pieces of corn out of our bag because we believe that in some way, He will turn each piece of corn into a piece of gold.

As we can see, this is a story about generosity. Although most of us want to be more generous, it can be difficult to figure out what the Lord is asking of us. Then, once we think we know what we are being ask to do, it can take a lot of courage to do it. In other words, it takes courage to become more generous.

When I was younger, I always thought about generosity in terms of quantity. You did *more* of something. To be generous with your life of prayer, you prayed more. If you were trying to be more generous in living a virtuous life, you tried to practice a particular virtue more. If you wanted to be more generous in a life of service, you spent more time at it. Or, you became involved in more things.

I don't think this way about generosity anymore. You see, when I was younger, I didn't have much life experience. And, I didn't have much wisdom then either. But now that I am older and hopefully, somewhat wiser, I have come to understand the richness of this idea of generosity in a much broader way. It is true that sometimes generosity still continues to mean giving *more* of something. But it is much richer than that. And I think this is what Jesus was trying to teach the apostles with the story of the widow's mite in chapter 12 of Mark's Gospel. She didn't have very much. But what she had, she generously shared.

The late Jesuit theologian Karl Rahner, wrote about the richness of generosity. He called it giving *the more*. Rahner believed that the Lord is always inviting us to grow in a life of generosity, to give the more. But this can mean so many different things to people depending on what is happening in their lives. And the *more* for us will certainly change as we journey through life. But whatever it is that we are asked to do, however we are invited to become more generous, will always require more courage. For the rich young man in the Gospels, the more was to give up his riches and come follow Jesus. This would take courage. But we know from his response that he wasn't ready to do this and so, he walked away sad (Luke 18: 18–23). However, Jesus didn't go after him trying to convince him to come back. He knew this person wasn't ready for this challenge at this point in his life. He lacked the courage to make the changes that would be required for a new life style in order to follow the Lord more closely. And what about that poor widow in Mark's Gospel? The more for her was to give the little she had. When we see the response of Jesus, it was like he used this as a teaching moment as he said to his disciples "come over here and see what generosity is all about. It is not a matter of giving *a lot* of anything." Rather, "truly I tell you, this poor widow has put in more than all those who are contributing to the treasury. For all of them have contributed out of their abundance; but she out of her poverty has put in everything she had, all she had to live on" (Mark 12: 41–44). Generosity is not measured in terms of quantity. It is so much more than that.

So, what might this mean for each of us? What does giving *the more* mean in our daily lives? For each of us, there are so many opportunities to give of ourselves in so many ways. These are invitations to become more generous. We will discover what the Lord is asking of us, what it is that we might take out of our bag of life, in our time of prayer and in our moments of solitude. In these moments, we might discover that it involves giving away our time to help someone, using a skill we have, patiently listening to someone, saying hello, offering a smile to someone who looks like they might be having a bad day, calling someone who is hurting or grieving, sending a card to a friend, volunteering at some organization, or emailing someone who needs some helpful information. There are so many ways to give of ourselves. So many ways to be generous. So many ways to give *the more*. And as we pray for the strength to have the courage to share what we have like the widow in Mark's Gospel, we do so believing that the Lord *will* turn our efforts into pieces of gold.

Conclusion

SOME YEARS AGO, I heard a story about a lady who volunteered at a shelter for abused children. One day, this lady met a boy named Billy. He had been terribly wounded and was reluctant to go beyond the security he had found in his room. The day of the Christmas party, he shrank against the pillow on his bed and refused to leave his room. "But aren't you coming to the party?" the lady asked. He shook his head. "Sure you are," said another volunteer beside me. "All you need is to put on your courage skin." His eye brows went up. He thought for a moment. "Okay," he finally said. While the lady watched, the other volunteer helped him don an imaginary suit of "courage skin," and off he went to the party, willing to risk leaving the secure place of his room.

Like Billy, courage will always require that we leave some secure place within ourselves and step out into the unknown. But if, like Billy, we can put on our courage skin, it will allow us to be courageous in many different ways. Sometimes, our courage will be known and seen by others. Often, it will only be known and experienced by ourselves. But this doesn't matter at all. In the final analysis, it will be one of our quiet, hidden faces of courage in which we are doing our part to become the person God wants us to be and trying to influence life in a positive way. Let's put on our "courage skin," and get busy!

Bibliography

Albom, Mitch. *Tuesdays with Morrie: An Old Man, A Young Man, and Life's Greatest Lesson.* New York: Doubleday, 1997.
Aristotle. *Nicomachean Ethics.* Book II, chapter 1.
Brown, Brene. *The Gifts of Imperfection.* City Center, MN: Hazelden Publishing, 2010.
Brown, Stuart and Vaughan, Christopher. *Play: How It Shapes the Brain, Opens the Imagination, and Invigorates the Soul.* New York: Penguin Group, 2009.
Coles, Robert. *Dorothy Day: A Radical Devotion.* Reading, MA: Perseus, 1987.
DeMello, Anthony. *The Heart of the Enlightened.* New York: Doubleday, 1989.
Germer, Christopher. *The Mindful Path to Self-Compassion: Freeing Yourself from Destructive Thoughts and Emotions.* New York: Guilford Press, 2009.
Gilkey, Langdon. *Naming the Whirlwind.* New York: The Bobbs Merrill Co., 1969.
Goleman, Daniel. *Social Intelligence: The New Science of Human Relationships.* New York: Random House, 2006.
Goodall, Jane. *Reason for Hope: A Spiritual Journey.* New York: Warner, 1999.
Hammarskjold, Dag. *Markings.* London: Faber and Faber, 1963.
Hanh, Thich Nhat. *Living Buddha, Living Christ.* New York: Penguin, 1995.
Hollis, James. *Living an Examined Life.* Boulder, CO: Sounds True, Inc., 2018.
Jones, Alan. *Journey into Christ.* San Francisco: Harper & Row, 1971.
Jung, Carl. *The Structure and Dynamics of the Psyche. Collected Works of C. G. Jung 8.* Translated by R. F. C. Hull. New Jersey: Princeton University Press, 1960.
Kea, Elizabeth. *Amazed by Grace.* Nashville: Thomas Nelson, 2003.
Keating, Thomas. *The Heart of the World.* New York: Crossroads, 2008.
Mahalik, James. "Development of the Conformity to Feminine Norms Inventory." *Sex Roles,* 52 no. 7–8, (2005), 417–35.
May, Rollo. *The Courage to Create.* New York: Bantam, 1975.
Melville, Herman. *Moby Dick.* New York: Charles Scribner's Sons, 1902.
Miles, Sara. *Jesus Freak: Feeding, Healing, Raising the Dead.* San Francisco: Jossey-Boss, 2010.
McCain, John. *Why Courage Matters.* New York: Random House, 2004.
Neff, Kristin. "Self-Compassion: An Alternative Conceptualization of a Healthy Attitude Toward Oneself." *Self and Identity,* 2, (2003), 223–50.
Nouwen, Henri. *The Road to Daybreak: A Spiritual Journey.* New York: Image Books, 1990.
Rilke, Rainer Maria. *Letters to a Young Poet.* New York: Norton, 1934.
Satir, Virginia. *The Family Networker.* 13, (January–February), 28–32.
Shea, John. *Stories of God: An Unauthorized Biography.* Chicago: Thomas Moore, 1978.

Bibliography

Watson, David. "Embodiment, Vulnerability, and Relationships," *Weavings,* February, 2016, 21–25.

Weil, Simone. *First and Last Notebooks.* Translated by Richard Rees. New York: Oxford University Press, 1970.

Zee, Ginger. *Natural Disaster: I Cover Them. I am One.* Los Angeles: Kingswell, 2017.

www.ingramcontent.com/pod-product-compliance
Lightning Source LLC
Chambersburg PA
CBHW070921160426
43193CB00011B/1546